AF260763

3

Integrity Publishing International LLC

Copyright © 2026

Published by Integrity Publishing International LLC
www.IntegrityPub.com

FAITH IN MOTION | MICHELLE MRAS

Orders by U.S. trade bookstores and wholesalers.

Email: *Team@IntegrityPub.com*

Paperback ISBN: 978-1-964330-38-9

MICHELLE MRAS

HD. Global Keynote Speaker . Executive Speaker Coach

FAITH
IN MOTION

13-STEP SURVIVOR'S GUIDE TO THRIVING IN YOUR LIFE

FOREWORD &
ACKNOWLEDGEMENT
BY ERIK SWANSON

I would like to personally acknowledge and thank the one and only Napoleon Hill for his work, dedication, and, most importantly, his belief in himself. Whether he realized this or not, his unwavering belief in himself was passed down from generation to generation to millions and millions of individuals across this planet, including me!

I'm sure, at first, as many of us experience throughout our lives as well, he most likely had his doubts. Think about it. Being offered to work for Andrew Carnegie for a full 20 years with zero pay and no guarantee of success had to be a daunting decision. But, I thank you for making that decision years and years ago. It paved the way for countless people who trusted in themselves and found success in their rights. You gave us all hope, desire, and faith to bank on the most important energy in the world—ourselves!

For this, I thank you, Sir, from the bottom of my heart and the top of all of our bank accounts. Let us all follow the 13 Steps to Riches and prosper in so many areas of our lives.

~ Erik "Mr. Awesome" Swanson | Multi Time #1 Bestselling Author, TEDx and Harvard Speaker & Student of Napoleon Hill Philosophies

CONTENTS

INTRODUCTION

Have you ever looked into the night sky and pondered, "Why am I here?" Most of my life, I made a ritual of asking the stars that very question. As a young child in the Philippines, I would sit with my Lolo, aka Grandfather, and dream about what I wanted to be when I grew up. As the years passed, my question expanded to include, "Why is this happening to me?" These questions shaped who I am today, not because of the questions, but because of the answers I discovered while pondering and seeking answers to them.

Throughout my years of triumphs and tragedies, I have managed to set the very intentional goal of expanding my ability to grow, understand, accept, and ultimately love the person I am throughout my journey of returning to who I truly am. I used to ask, "Who am I becoming?" Now I know, this journey of life is designed for us to rediscover who we were before we were tainted by our environments, our circle of influences, and our fears of being unique.

When I was invited to share my perspectives on the principles of Napoleon Hill's *Think and Grow Rich*: Desire, Faith, Autosuggestion, Specialized Knowledge, Imagination, Organized Planning, Decision, Persistence, Power of the Mastermind, Sex Transmutation, the Subconscious Mind, the Brain and the Sixth Sense, through a series of books called *The*

13 Steps to Riches, I jumped at the opportunity. You see, through one of the toughest years of my life, I had a mentor who would loan me books to read. One such book was, Think and Grow Rich. I didn't quite grasp the verbiage and the power of the words in my late teens, but as an adult, I recognize how I would have been able to more efficiently navigate through my life, if I was able to grasp the concepts sooner.

I wrote my chapters for each of the principles for people like me, who need more relatable examples, and possibly a more feminine perspective. I understood each of the *Think and Grow Rich* principles at different points in my life. I didn't read it once and say, "Aha! I've got it, now I'm going to apply to my life." But, for the reader of my collected thought on the subjects, I shared why each principle presented itself in my life, how I used my past experiences and collected knowledge of the situation, and how the principle helped me realize my solutions. Then, how I used the principle to move forward.

Often, we can hear the same wisdom on repeat and still not grasp it. My hope for you, the reader of this book, is that my perspective is the voice your subconscious has been waiting to hear. I was told many years ago, "Someone is waiting for your voice." Perhaps you are my "someone". May my experiences encourage and ignite you to seek better tomorrows and to boldly step into being the best version of you, unapologetically.

— Dr. Michelle Mras

PROLOGUE BY DR. J.B. HILL

It was the last time that I would see Napoleon Hill alive. My father had taken his family for a three-day visit to Greenville, South Carolina. My sisters and I were in the back seat of the car, the driver's door was open, and my father was outside saying his goodbyes to his father, my grandfather, Napoleon Hill. Napoleon had three paperback copies of *Think and Grow Rich* in his hands. He leaned into the car and handed a copy to each of us. We quickly discovered a crisp, new ten-dollar bill, which my grandfather had enclosed with his autograph, boldly scrolled in bright green ink at the top of the title page.

He told us that ten dollars was the amount of money a man could earn in a day of hard labor and that we should remember this when we spent our money. He also told us to read his book. Dutifully, I complied, and although I enjoyed his storytelling style, my mind was not mature enough to understand it.

This changed over the course of a dozen years or so. I was lonely and had fallen into the habit of drifting through life. I had no money, no education, and no real skills. By chance, I found and bought a copy of my grandfather's book at a grocery store in North Carolina. This time, I was ready for his book, and, by reading it, I began to understand the value of what Napoleon Hill had placed in my hands. It was a recipe—a thirteen-step recipe for success. All I had to do was follow it—do what my grandfather told me to do. It worked: my life changed.

Many, many people have accomplished the same thing by following Napoleon's thirteen steps to success. One was Joe Dudley, who read *Think and Grow Rich* more than three hundred times. Dudley started life as the son of a tobacco sharecropper in North Carolina. He built a company valued at more than two hundred million dollars by selling products door-to-door. I asked him, "Why? Why would you read that book, any book, so often?" Dudley smiled and told me that reading it keeps his mind straight and that he learns something new with every read.

Bob Proctor read *Think and Grow Rich* every day of his adult life, and many other renowned people also attest to several readings. The most common reason given for this is to gain a deeper understanding of Hill's thinking. However, it is not necessary to read and re-read Hill's book to understand success more fully.

The 13 Steps to Riches does that for us. Each chapter is written by a well-known author with decades of experience reading and thinking about the steps to success. Therefore, *The 13 Steps to Riches* is synergistic in scope and a time-saver for serious students of success. It is certainly worth the read.

DR. JB HILL

Dr. James Blair Hill, known as Dr. J.B. Hill, was born in Morgantown, West Virginia, to David Hill, the youngest son of Napoleon Hill and Florence Hornor. Dr. Hill's journey embodies dedication, lifelong learning, and a commitment to serve, reflecting the values imparted by his grandfather, renowned author Napoleon Hill.

After graduating high school in 1966, Dr. Hill spent several years at sea on cargo ships. In 1969, he was drafted into the U.S. Marine Corps as a private, beginning a distinguished military career. He later pursued a bachelor's degree in mechanical engineering at Vanderbilt University, graduating in

1973 and earning a commission as a second lieutenant. As a field artillery officer in the Marines, Dr. Hill's discipline and drive led him to further academic achievements, including a Master's degree in Mathematics from the Naval Postgraduate School.

After 26 years of service, Dr. Hill retired from the Marine Corps in 1995. However, his desire to serve took him in a new direction—medicine. At the age of 53, he graduated from medical school, subsequently completing a three-year residency in family medicine. He was board-certified in Family Medicine and earned certifications in Wound Care and Hyperbaric Medicine. Today, he serves as a hospitalist in geriatric care, working to enhance the lives of elderly patients with compassion and expertise. He lives in Bridgeport, West Virginia, with his wife and two children.

Dr. Hill's connection to Napoleon Hill's philosophy was established early when, at the age of 12, his grandfather gifted him a copy of *Think and Grow Rich* with a simple yet profound directive: "Read it." Yet it wasn't until he was 23 that Dr. Hill grasped the full impact of his grandfather's teachings. This understanding became a cornerstone of his life, guiding him through challenges and instilling a sense of purpose that has defined his legacy in both his military and medical careers.

Through his life and work, Dr. Hill exemplifies the timeless principles of personal empowerment and service, leaving his own mark on a legacy that spans generations.

www.NapHill.org

GRAB YOUR COPY OF AN OFFICIAL PUBLICATION
WITH THE ORIGINAL UNEDITED TEXT FROM 1937
BY THE NAPOLEON HILL FOUNDATION!

THE NAPOLEON HILL FOUNDATION
WWW.NAPHILL.ORG

CHAPTER 1
IS YOUR GRASS GREEN

You've probably have heard the expression: "The grass is always greener on the other side of the fence". I learned early in life that the concept of "the grass is always greener" works regardless of which side of the fence you are on.

I was born in the late 1960s, the fourth child of a career United States Air Force military man. I spent my childhood in my mother's home country of the Philippines, where my father was stationed at Clark Air Base. My elder brothers and sister had lived in America before I was born. They told me stories of the grand cities and how different life was in the USA. I was a young American who had never seen America. To this point in my life, I had only experienced a tiny third-world country in the Pacific Ocean. I would look at the map of the world to compare the Philippine Islands to the United States. It baffled me that any land mass could be so vast.

My vision of American life was formed primarily by television, movies, and magazines. My naive view of American life fueled a large part of my childhood daydreams.

Imagine the rose-colored impression I held with views created from television shows like Leave it to Beaver, The Brady Bunch, The Courtship of Eddie's Father, The Carol Burnett Show and The Dick Van Dyke Show. My expectation of family life was that at the end of the day every mishap or situation would be settled. The house was always immaculately clean, organized, and dinner magically appeared out of the ovens fully garnished and ready to eat.

My glorified impression was amplified to spectacular heights through movies involving Elvis Presley, Gene Kelly, Fred Astaire, Judy Garland and the Rat Pack. The streets were clean, the buildings were spectacular, and if you were ever to break into song, everyone around you would sing along and dance in unison like a flash mob. Disney musicals created the additional bonus feature of animated creatures joining into the fun.

Magazines like Vogue, Woman's Day, Good Housekeeping and Reader's Digest further created images of beauty, glamour and insightfulness that fascinated my young mind. The women in America were glamorous, tall and nothing like me. They all looked like Barbie(™) dolls. Their flawless faces, big hair and graceful demeanor were not what I saw in my island world. Woman I knew were usually working hard, scrubbing, sweating, moving quickly through their activities, their hair up in makeshift buns with tendrils of stray hairs framing their sweat glistened faces.

The recipes in the magazines were always for huge pieces of meat with brightly colored side dishes. In the Philippines, we would have a much smaller portion of meat, usually cut into bite-sized pieces combined into large pots of savory goodness which incorporated vegetables along with a large side of steamed rice. I must admit, my impressions of American food did not surpass what I saw before me on a daily basis.

The stories, mysteries and jokes in Reader's Digest fueled the illusion that people in America were exciting, sleuth-like and light-hearted. I felt as if I was missing out. I would hear fabulous stories and sample yummy stateside treats provided by the other school children who would visit grandparents over the Summer breaks and newly transferred students. My desire to see this magical land was relentless.

You may wonder how anyone would believe what they saw in television, movies, or magazines to be true? Let me explain. In the Philippines, the people on local television looked like people you would meet on the streets. The movies tend to be dramas about life of which I saw on (almost) a daily basis. The magazines showed Filipinos in real life situations, and even though the models were pretty, they didn't look store bought dolls. From what I saw about America, it was a representation of what life was truly like.

In 1975, my dreams became a reality. My family was reassigned to Louisiana in the deep South of the United States. My airline flight was exhilarating! The stewardesses and pilots fit my expectations of real Americans - statuesque airline attendants along with pilots who seemed to have perfectly chiseled features. I excused their lack of dancing and singing to the small space within the plane. After we reached America, I distinctly remember being confused of where all the border lines, state colors, blue water features and terrain features were as I gazed out the window to the America below. I didn't see one map feature below us. The lack of topographical features should have been an indication that my glamorized view of America would not be as expected. When we landed in Louisiana, my sister and I were sent to call our grandmother's house to let her know we arrived. This was another eye opening adventure. In the Philippines, we had operators that monitor the phone lines. My sister picked up the phone handle prepared to ask the operator to connect her to the number written on the piece of paper our mother had handed her. There was no voice, no assistance. Puzzled, we examined the phone booth, read the directions to insert a coin and dialed our Grandmother's number. The next befuddlement occurred as I gazed around the terminal to see hundreds of tired, disheveled and agitated people scattered around a hot, dirty and noisy airport. This was not the clean, bright and shiny American experience I expected and I still had not witnessed one group song or dance routine!

I discovered more misconceptions once we arrived at our Grandmother's house and followed her into the kitchen. Grandma asked me to go to the freezer to get her an ingredient. When I opened it, I was astonished to discover it was a whole refrigerator devoted to left-overs! In the Philippines, there was no thoughts of storing food for months. Whatever was left over from one meal became part of the next meal.

America was quite different from life in the Philippines. As the days passed, I realized that what I saw and based my desire to come to America was based upon the Hollywood versions of life in America, not real life. Gradually, I learned to appreciate the less than idealistic version of what life was like in America. I saw similarities and many differences to the life I grew up knowing. Experiencing life as an American in America was a fantastic learning experience. Within two-years, my father's job returned our family to Clark Air Base, Philippines. My excitement and desire to return to the country I called home was based with the knowledge that although our little island country didn't have all the advantages and conveniences of American life, it was a less complicated and a happy way to live.

The lessons I learned during this point of my young life guided me into adulthood. Whenever I desired a particular standard of living, an experience, relationship, etc. I take the time to study, examine and see the opportunity or experience from multiple points of views. Then I ask myself: Will I be disappointed if it does not meet my expectations? What will I do to adjust to the reality of the outcome? How will I react? Do I truly desire what I pursue or can I adjust what I currently have? A strong desire for something creates expectations of a "grass being greener" scenario. I learned creating that image of what you want is beneficial. Just be sure to be prepared for what reality may bring. What I thought I wanted was bigger, brighter and more. I learned to appreciate the simpler, laid back island life. Desire is based on what you don't have. You don't know what you've got until it's gone.

MOTIVATION BY DESIRE

Positive self-motivation is the inner drive that keeps you moving forward in pursuit of your goals. Winners in every field in the game of life are driven by desire. There never has been a consistent winner in any profession who didn't have that burning desire to win… internalized. Although the Scriptures have preached it as a basic axiom in life for centuries, this concept was first presented in the self-improvement industry by Earl Nightingale in his platinum audio recording of "The Strangest Secret." The strangest secret is that we become what we think about most of the time. In other words, we and our children are motivated every day and moved by our current dominant thoughts. We are moved in the direction of what we dwell on. We can't concentrate on the reverse of an idea. Everyone in life is self-motivated, positively or negatively. Even a decision to do nothing is a decision based on motivation.

In the field of psychology, we make a basic distinction between intrinsic and extrinsic motivation. Having intrinsic motivation means doing something for its own sake., like playing a sport just for the joy of playing. On the other hand, extrinsic motivation pulls you by the power of some external benefit or tangible reward you'll attain by taking action, as in the case of a professional athlete who plays primarily for money rather than for the fun or challenge of the sport. It also influences people in their business careers, especially among those who are driven fundamentally by the income they receive rather than by the love of the service they provide.

Motivation is a highly emotional state and the great physical and mental motivators in life such as survival and love are filled with emotion. And the two key emotions which dominate all human motivation, with opposite, but nearly equally effective results, are fear and desire. Fear, of course, is the most powerful, negative motivator of all. Fear is the great dictator, that forces us to do things that we feel we have to do because of the consequences. Fear is the great inhibitor, the red light that tells us that we can't do things, because of the obstacles and risks.

Through the years I've been telling the story of a man who may unwittingly have become a victim of his own negative premonition, a kind of self-inflicted voodoo spell. It was a true account of a man named, Nick Sitzman, a strong, healthy individual who worked as a yardman for a railroad company in Omaha, Nebraska. According to his supervisor, Nick was a good worker who got along fine with his fellow workers and was reliable on the job. He had one noticeable fault, however. He was a notorious worrier. He was cynical about everything and usually feared the worst about the world situation, the economy, the weather and the future, in general.

One summer day, the train crews were informed that they could quit an hour early in honor of the foreman's birthday.

Accidentally, Nick was locked in an empty, isolated refrigerator boxcar, in which he had been working, that was in the yard for repairs, and the rest of the workmen left the site. Nick panicked. He banged and shouted until his fists were raw and his voice hoarse. No one paid any attention. If they heard him, they associated the sound with a playground nearby or with the noise of other trains backing in and out of the yard.

"Hey, let me out of here, it must be zero degrees in this refrigerator car," he must have thought. "If I can't get out soon, I'll freeze to death." He found a cardboard box and, shivering uncontrollably, he scrawled this message to his wife and family: "So cold, body is getting numb. If I could just go to sleep. These may be my last words."

The next morning, the crew slid open the heavy doors of the boxcar and found Nick dead. An autopsy revealed that every physical sign in his body indicated he had frozen to death. But the irony was that the refrigeration unit was inoperative and there was plenty of fresh air in the boxcar. It was a mild summer afternoon and evening, with the temperature inside steady at about sixty-one degrees. His fear motivation became a self-fulfilling prophecy.

As a positive power, belief becomes the promise of the realization of things hoped for and unseen. As a negative power, it is the premonition of our deepest fears and unseen darkness. A self-fulfilling prophecy perhaps can be best defined as a statement or concept that is not necessarily true nor false, but is capable of becoming true if it is believed and internalized.

Desire is like a strong, positive magnet. It beckons and welcomes us toward our goals. Fear usually looks through the rear view mirror at missed opportunities and problems and with apprehension to the future.

Fear breeds compulsion. Desire creates positive propulsion. Fear breeds inhibition. Desire triggers ignition power. Winners have learned how to concentrate on the desired results, rather than possible problems. And winners dwell on the rewards of success, instead of the penalties of failure.

THE LAW OF ATTRACTION TAKES ACTION

Over a decade ago, I participated in the video and book project called "The Secret", based upon the Law of Attraction. One way or another, our actions cause rewards and consequences. "To every action," as Sir Isaac Newton observed, "there is always opposed an equal reaction." Good begets good and evil leads to more evil. This is one of the universe's eternal, fundamental truths which I have referred to as The Unfailing Boomerang or the Law of Cause and Effect.

It means that every cause (action) will create an effect (reaction) approximately equal in intensity. Making good use of our minds, skills, and talents will bring positive rewards in our outer lives. Assuming the personal responsibility to make the best use of our talents and time will result in an enormous gain in happiness, success, and wealth. This is true of everyone.

The truly successful winners, those who have built financial empires or accomplished great deeds for society, are those who have taken personal responsibility to heart and to soul. By being true to themselves and others, they achieve success, wealth, and inner happiness. In the end, we ourselves--far more than any outsider--are the people with the greatest ability to steal our own time, talents, and accomplishments.

I'm fond of a story from the Old Testament Book of Leviticus about a sacred ceremony called "The Escaped Goat." When the people's troubles became overwhelming in those early days, a healthy male goat was led into the temple. The tribe's highest priest placed his hand on the animal's head and solemnly recited the long list of the people's woes. Then the goat was released--and it ran off, supposedly taking the human troubles and evil spirits with him. That was some four thousand years ago, but the concept of the scapegoat remains in full force today. Blaming someone else or something else for our problems is nearly as old as civilization--and stays consistently young. When Adam ate of the apple, he quickly pointed at Eve. "The woman you've put here with me made me do it," he said.

We live in a land of incredible abundance. Americans enjoy material riches and a civic and legal inheritance that people of other countries continue to die for. We protest for individual liberty and social order in the same breath. We strive for material wealth, hoping that spiritual riches will come with it as a bonus. We plead for more protection from crime but demand less interference in our social habits. We want to cut taxes and build our own empires--at the same time, we want our government to provide more financial security. But we can't have it both ways. If we want results, we must pay the price.

Life's greatest risk is depending on others for your security, which can really come only by planning, acting, and making choices that will make you independent.

> *There was a very cautious man,*
> *Who never laughed or played;*
> *He never risked, he never tried,*
> *He never sang or prayed.*
> *And when he one day passed away,*
> *His insurance was denied;*
> *For since he really never lived,*
> *They claimed he never died.*

There are two primary choices in our lives: to accept conditions as they exist or to assume the responsibility for changing them. The price of success includes taking responsibility for giving up bad habits and invalid assumptions; setting a worthy example in our own lives; leading ourselves and others down a new and unfamiliar path; working more to reach a goal and being willing to delay gratification along the way; distancing ourselves from a peer group that isn't helping us succeed and therefore tends or wants to hold us back; and being willing to face criticism and jealousy from people who would like to keep us stuck in place with them.

My decades of research have convinced me that the happiest, best-adjusted individuals in their present and older lives are those who believe they have a strong measure of control over their lives. They seem to choose more appropriate responses to what occurs and to stand up to inevitable changes with less apprehension. They learn from their past mistakes, rather than replay them. They spend time "doing" in the present, rather than fearing what may happen. So, stop stewing and start doing. If the pandemic has taught us anything, it is that we must b prepared for sudden change and surprises on a daily basis. Being resilient in turbulent times is our new reality.

ACTION TNT: TODAY NOT TOMORROW

My grandfather owned a bookstore and bindery in San Diego where I used to work on weekends as a pre-teen and teenager. In addition to gluing books together and sweeping out his store, I loved browsing and sampling the stacks of books on the shelves. It was like a candy store of wisdom to me. He had a poster on the wall that I copied in my notebook because my grandpa said it was an important lesson for me to learn when I was young. He said procrastination is a favorite hiding place for people who are afraid to risk making mistakes, which is why he almost never put off any important decisions regarding the family. I have memorized that poster and refer to it often when I spend time puttering, majoring in minors and doing meaningless activities that are tension-relieving instead of goal achieving. The title is simply—Tomorrow:

He was going to be what he wanted to be—tomorrow. None would be kinder and braver than he—tomorrow. A friend who was troubled and weary he knew, who'd be glad for a lift and needed it too, on him he would call and see what he could do – tomorrow. Each morning he'd stack up the letters he'd write— tomorrow. And thought of the clients he'd fill with delight— tomorrow. But he hadn't a minute to stop on his way, "More time I will give to others," he'd say—"tomorrow." The greatest of leaders this man would have been—tomorrow. The world would have hailed him had he ever seen—tomorrow. But in fact, he passed on, and he faded from view. And all that he left here when his life was through, was a mountain of things he intended to do—TOMORROW.

MOTIVATION INTO MOTIVE-ACTION

Here are some motivation actions you can take to reach your goals instead of letting fear and negativity keep you in a constant state of frustration and anxiety:

1. Remember: we become what we think about. What the mind harbors, the body manifests in some way. Focus your mind, which I call your software program) on your desired goals that you want your brain and body (your hard-drive and hardware) to achieve.

2. View failure as target correction. Failure is only a detour, not a dead end. The person interested in success has to learn to view failure as a healthy, inevitable part of the process of getting to the top. I look at failure as the fertilizer of success. Don't roll in it. Use the experience as growth material. So make a pact with yourself. I suggest you write an agreement with yourself. Promise that you won't allow a failure to be more than a learning experience that allows you to move more quickly to the place you want to be.

3. Keep your self-talk affirmative. Whether you're at work, at home or on the golf course or tennis court, your subconscious is recording every word. Instead of "should have" say "will do." Instead of "if only" say "next time." Instead of "Yes, but" say "Why not?" Instead of "problem" say "opportunity." Instead of "difficult" say "challenging." "Instead of "could have" say "My goal." Instead of "Someday" say "Today." Say "In the hole, before you putt on the green while playing golf, and "First serve in" when it's your serve on the tennis court.

4. Forget perfection. Only the saints are perfect—and "Sainthood is acceptable only in saints." Accept the flaws and count your blessings instead of your blemishes.

5. Declare a moratorium on negatives—negative thoughts, negative people, negative forms of entertainment. Keep your desire to succeed strong by erasing thoughts of the downside. To win you must continuously motivate yourself toward your goals. And you must be willing to do this yourself.

6. Be willing to say to yourself, "I'm on the right road. I'm doing OK. I'm succeeding." We too frequently become adept at identifying our flaws and failures. Become equally adept at recognizing your achievements. What are you doing now that you weren't doing one month ago … six months ago … a year ago. What habits have changed? Chart your progress.

Doing well once or twice is relatively easy. Real winning is continuously moving ahead. Winning is tough, in part, because it is so easy to revert to old habits and former lifestyles. Over the long run, you need to give yourself regular feedback and monitor your performance. Reinforce yourself positively to stay on track. Don't wait for an award ceremony, promotion, friend or mentor to show appreciation for your work. Do it yourself! Do it now. Take pride in your own efforts on a daily basis.

7. Set up a dynamic daily routine. Getting into a positive routine or groove, instead of a negative rut, will help you become more effective. Why is the subway the most energy efficient means of transportation? Because it runs on a track. Think of the order in your day, instead of the routine. Don't worry about sameness, neatness or everything exactly in its place. Order is being able to do what you really choose and not taking on more than you can manage. Order frees you up. Get into the swing of a healthy, daily routine and discover how much more control you'll gain in your life.

Here are 5 keys to adding order to a winning routine:

Simplify – challenge complicated plans or processes.

Don't spend a lot of time searching for things – you probably don't need them anyway.

Do what you promise to do – and promise only what you can do
Set effective agendas with others ahead of time – so neither of you is disappointed.

Monitor yourself in order to make sure you accomplish what you set out to do.
And remember:

Change your attitude and lifestyle, and many of your outcomes will change automatically. Because you are an uncut gemstone of priceless value. Cut and polish your potential with knowledge, skills and service and you will be in great demand throughout your life. Optimists rule the future. Imagination and innovation flourish when nations, companies, teams, families and individuals are motivated by the rewards of success, instead of the penalties of failure. Fear compels and inhibits. Desire is that burning fire of hope within that turns dreams into reality. Ask any athlete training for 1200 days for an opportunity to be an Olympian, what motivates her or him. It is the torch of passion.

38

DR. DENIS WAITLEY

Denis Waitley has inspired, informed, challenged, and entertained audiences for over 25 years, from the boardrooms of multi-national corporations to the locker rooms of world-class athletes and in the meeting rooms of thousands of conventioneers throughout the world. Recently, he was voted business speaker of the year by the Sales and Marketing Executives Association and by Toastmasters International and inducted into the International Speakers Hall of Fame.

With over 10 million audio programs sold in 14 languages, Denis Waitley is one of the most listened-to voices on personal and career success. He is the author of 16 non-fiction books, including several International bestsellers, *Seeds of Greatness*, *Being the Best*, *The Winners' Edge*, *The Joy of Working*, and *Empire of the Mind.*

His audio album, *The Psychology of Winning*, is the all-time bestselling program on self-mastery.

Denis Waitley has studied and counseled winners in every field, from Apollo astronauts to Super Bowl champions, from sales achievers to government leaders and youth groups.

During the 1980s, he served as Chairman of Psychology on the U.S. Olympic Committee's Sports Medicine Council, responsible for the performance enhancement of all U.S. Olympic athletes.

Denis Waitley is a founding director of the National Council on Self-Esteem and the President's Council on Vocational Education, and recently received the "Youth Flame Award" from the National Council on Youth Leadership for his outstanding contribution to high school youth leadership.

As President of the International Society for Advanced Education, inspired by Dr. Jonea Salk, he counseled returning POWs from Vietnam and conducted simulation and stress management seminars for Apollo astronauts.

41

CHAPTER 2

YOU'RE NOT DEAD YET—GET UP!

Have you ever taken the time to watch a toddler at the early stages of walking? They pull themselves up by grabbing furniture, pant legs, or any object that appears larger than themselves. They rely on their strength while holding Faith, per se, in the object they use to become upright. We watch them, smile, and have admiration for their tenacity.

It was May 2014 when my lesson of embracing the tenacity of a toddler became the catalyst of what I believe saved my life. Prior to then, I was living the life I perceived to be expected of me. I was an above-average student, played sports, had a large group of friends, attended college to get an engineering degree, married my high school sweetheart, became a mother, kept our home practically perfect, and made well-rounded meals every day. I maintained an overactive level of participation in our children's school activities, baking cookies, and working every event possible, all while maintaining a job outside of the home. I was in full Wonder Woman mode until I wasn't.

On that auspicious day in May, I was in an automobile accident that left me with what we thought was a slight concussion. Twelve days after the accident, I lost my ability to form sentences and, shortly afterward, the ability to walk without assistance. My life changed forever. I went from doing everything to needing assistance to wash and feed myself. I was on a regime of pain killers and brain therapies. After a year spent trapped in this state of being, I discovered that I had a Traumatic Brain Injury (TBI) that affected four areas of my brain. The therapy to have my brain communicate more effectively increased. I was fully cognizant inside my mind without the ability to communicate through writing or speech.

Every time I showed signs of improvement, something would occur, and my brain would lock down again. This was my idea of Hell. I became severely depressed because of the lack of independence and the increased inner-critic thoughts that bombarded me daily with all my shortcomings. I had lost Faith in God and the possibility of ever regaining any semblance of who I was. That is when the suicidal thoughts joined the chorus.

My ability to recognize the passing of time had also left me, but I distinctly remember sitting on my couch. I was guided there every morning by a family member. I would remain there until someone came home to move me or feed me. This particular day, I was alone. I meticulously played suicide scenarios through my mind. I became increasingly agitated because all plans I concocted were undoable simply due to the fact I couldn't move without help. In frustration, I screamed in my mind to God, "If you hate me so much, kill me already!" to which I heard the response, "You're not dead yet, get up."

I don't know if you have ever had an experience like that, but I assure you, it was a voice you cannot ignore. It reverberated throughout every cell in my body and through every molecule around me. When I heard the command, I saw myself in every moment in my life when I had felt abandoned or left to suffer as if they were movie scenes. In each instance, I was held by an unseen hand. To this day, I can't honestly explain it in words. I felt a wave of peace and acceptance wash over me. The next thing I knew, I was on my knees in the middle of the living room, several feet from my couch. I was saying, "Thank you for every experience. Thank you for my life."

When my husband returned home, he found me sitting at the office computer, insisting that I needed to speak. He said, "How are you speaking? How did you move to the office?" Two activities entirely out of my abilities for the past two years. Yet, there I was.

My journey to the woman I am today was not instantaneous. I had fantastic days and very challenging days. There were times I could perform daily tasks without assistance and others when I couldn't leave my bed for weeks. I would walk, then have vertigo attacks. Pull up, then fall. Speak coherent sentences, then revert to playing charades to ask for water. Recovery was not easy nor was it linear.

I found a renewed love for life. I stopped viewing the challenges before me as punishments for my inadequacies. Instead, I considered the challenges to be circumvented and conquered. I smiled through my pain, not because it didn't hurt.

I smiled because I had the gift of waking up to complain. I laughed at my shortcomings and figured out other ways to complete a task. In short, I had reverted my mindset to that of a toddler.

Every day I become better. I still have days when I can feel my brain's short circuit, and that's okay. It simply means I need to throttle back and approach my day differently. It has become part of my life to adjust and reset.

How about you? Do you allow circumstances, situations, and people to throw your day off? Do you get frustrated when what you expect to happen doesn't? How about when someone doesn't do what you want them to do? Do you get frustrated with yourself?

There is a quote by Byron Katie that comes to me daily. It reads, "There are only three kinds of business in the universe: mine, yours, and God's." Control what is in your sphere of control—YOU. How does this quote guide me daily? How can it guide you to success? Whenever you feel overwhelmed or unable to control a situation, ask yourself, "Who am I attempting to control?" Once you realize the answer isn't, "Myself," back off.

Faith comes into play throughout every aspect of life's ups and downs. In my experience, I lost Faith in God and in myself. That lack of belief kept me from getting back up. Once I realized I am not alone, my confidence rejuvenated. I had my much-needed preverbal object to hold on to when I felt unstable and ready to fall. Now, when I fall, I have the tenacity of a toddler to do everything within my power to find a way back up. I have Faith in myself that there is a way.

I found that the key to getting back up after a pitfall is to keep Faith in God or a higher power while maintaining confidence in yourself. Throughout my TBI journey, I have met many individuals who are experiencing life challenges. They wonder why they aren't recovering or are more successful. They have Faith in God or a higher power, but they lack confidence in themselves. To move to your next level, be it health, relationships, career, etc., you must have Faith in both.

My mentor, Paul Scheele of Scheele Learning Strategies, shared an observation that holds regardless of your stage of life. "We, as humans, are created to fall. From the time we learn to walk, we fall, we get back up, we fall again, we get back up. We are designed to fall and get back up." The importance of falling is to learn from the fall, adjust to repeat what worked, and not repeat what doesn't. You must have Faith that you will find a way.

Remember that you are a toddler in an adult body. You will fall. Train yourself to have Faith that there is something more significant than holding on and holding Faith that you can adapt and learn no matter what you desire to accomplish. Embrace your toddler mindset and "Get up. You're not dead yet."

EXCERPT BY SHARON LECHTER

HAVE YOU ADDED VALUE INTO SOMEONE'S LIFE TODAY?

What role has FAITH played in your life and in your success? Try to remember a time when you "powered through" a difficult period in your life. How did FAITH show up and help you through?

When I asked myself this question, I first think about the spiritual aspect of faith and my trust in a higher power… but I also think about the faith I have in myself. It reminds me of my father and a simple question he would ask me each night.

"HAVE YOU ADDED VALUE TO SOMEONE'S LIFE TODAY?"

My dad used to ask me that question every night when I was growing up. He has been gone for 15 years, but I still ask myself this same question every evening.

As a child, I didn't understand how dramatically this simple question would impact my life. By concentrating on adding value to others' lives, you don't focus on just yourself or your personal desires. But even more importantly, when you see the positive impact your actions make in the lives of others, it makes you feel better about yourself. It builds your self-confidence, or faith in yourself by helping others find faith in themselves. That is truly adding value to the world.

When most people hear the word faith, they think of faith from a spiritual perspective. Spiritual faith in God or a higher power is incredibly important and creates a fundamental belief system that shapes who we are and who we become as adults.

It is also important not to neglect the faith that we can build in ourselves and in each other every single day through the thoughts, words and actions that we choose. I realize that the nightly question from my father and my desire to help others helped me build faith and self-confidence as a result of my service to others.

In addition to spiritual faith and faith in yourself you can have faith in others, faith in your endeavors and faith that you will succeed.

WHAT IS THE FIRST THOUGHT THE WORD FAITH TRIGGERS IN YOUR MIND?

Many of history's greatest thought leaders have highlighted the importance of faith.

Faith consists in believing when it is beyond the power of reason to believe.
~ Voltaire

He who has faith has... an inward reservoir of courage, hope, confidence, calmness, and assuring trust that all will come out well—even though to the world it may appear to come out most badly. B. C. Forbes (founder of Forbes Magazine)

Faith is the strength by which a shattered world shall emerge into the light.
~ Helen Keller

When you focus on being a blessing, God makes sure that you are always blessed in abundance.
~ Joel Osteen

In faith there is enough light for those who want to believe and enough shadows to blind those who don't.
~ Blaise Pascal

Keep your dreams alive. Understand to achieve anything requires faith and belief in yourself, vision, hard work, determination, and dedication. Remember all things are possible for those who believe.
~ Gail Devers

In *Think and Grow Rich*, Napoleon Hill himself challenged the notion that faith is only about religious belief. Faith becomes the beacon of light that provides a path forward and engages your subconscious mind. Without faith, negativity fills your subconscious and multiplies more negativity. On the other hand, optimism, positivity, and faith create the foundation that shields your mind from negativity and from which success can be built.

Let's review Hill's definition of FAITH and the role it plays in creating success in your life:

HAVE FAITH IN YOURSELF: FAITH IN THE INFINITE

FAITH is the "external elixir" which gives life, power, and action to the impulse of thought!
FAITH is the starting point of all accumulation of riches!
FAITH is the basis of all "miracles" and all mysteries which cannot be analyzed by the rules of science!
FAITH is the only known antidote for FAILURE!
FAITH is the element, the "chemical" which, when mixed with prayer, gives one direct communication with Infinite Intelligence.
FAITH is the element which transforms the ordinary vibration of thought, created by the finite mind of man, into the spiritual equivalent.
FAITH is the only agency through which the cosmic force of Infinite Intelligence can be harnessed and used by man.

The importance of faith became very clear to me during the writing process for *Three Feet From Gold*, my first *Think and Grow Rich* series book with the Napoleon Hill Foundation co-authored with Greg Reid. As we interviewed successful business men and women, we found they shared common traits that drove them to success. But even more importantly we found the common attributes that helped them drive and persevere through the tough times.. turning obstacles they faced into opportunities. As a result of our research we formulated the Personal Success Equation to share the common elements of their success stories.

It is as follows:

[(P + T) x A x A] + F = Personal Success Equation
[(**P**assion + **T**alent) x **A**ssociation x **A**ction] + **F**aith = Personal Success Equation

Just as Hill discovered the principles of success by research and study of the most successful people of his time and shared them in *Think and Grow Rich*, the personal success equation was derived by analysis of what was key to the success of modern industry leaders and their ability to overcome obstacles. When you combine your **P**assion and your **T**alent with the right **A**ssociations and then take the right **A**ctions you are well on your way to success. Your Passion and Talents are personal to you, often learned in school or from life experience. But true success is achieved through the Power of Association and taking action towards your goals. And we almost went to print with *Three Feet From Gold* with that as the formula but I recognized that a huge common element with these industry leaders that was missing was their incredible Faith. Faith in themselves, faith in what they were doing, faith that it was needed and necessary and faith that they would succeed. That faith kept them moving and persevering even during tough times when others would have easily quit "three feet from gold!"

In addition, we discovered that for many business owners that "F" actually stood for Fear, not Faith. And it was that Fear that make it easy for them to give up and quit, choosing NOT to persevere. This fear prevented them from achieving the success they deserved.

It is impossible to have Faith and Fear in your mind at the same time. Having faith helps you keep fear under control. Fear does one of two things - it paralyzes us or motivates us. The vast majority of us are paralyzed by fear so we fail to take action. We hide away and isolate and end up missing opportunities that are right there in front of us. This fear stops us and keeps us from moving past the obstacle that caused the fear.

When we internalize that fear it becomes destructive. We start thinking things like, "I am not good enough, I am not qualified, I am not thin enough, I am just not as lucky as he is." In each of these statements we are giving up our own power and judging ourselves through the eyes of others. This negativity eats away at our self-confidence and destroys our faith in ourselves. If we can learn to identify the fear and turn it into energy and action, we can overcome it, stand tall in our own power and place ourselves in the position of greatest potential.

Hill provides us with a roadmap to overcome fear in *Outwitting the Devil*, which he actually wrote in 1938, intending it to be the sequel to *Think and Grow Rich*. But it was kept in a vault until I had to honor to annotate it and share it in 2015. (Why was it kept in the vault? His wife was afraid of the title!) In this manuscript, Hill provides incredible insights into why we hold ourselves back and fail to reach the level of success we deserve. He takes on every taboo of our times... sex, politics, education, religion, diet, alcohol, cigarettes just to name a few… and shares how fear manipulates us in each one of these areas and prevents us from achieving the success we deserve.

This fear robs us of the ability to think for ourselves. To have control over our own thoughts. He talks about fear of poverty, fear of death, fear of criticism, fear of old age, fear of loss of love. I believe the fear of criticism is pervasive in society today and prevents us from finding our own voice. We are so afraid of what others will think of us, of being embarrassed or being different that we "go with the flow" and don't carve our own path.

Outwitting the Devil shows you how to break the paralysis of fear and take control of your thoughts, your actions and your results. It all starts with Definiteness of Purpose. When you know what your definiteness of purpose is, it gives you courage and energy to move forward. Just as asking myself if I have added value to someone's life today does, it takes you out of yourself and allows you to focus on being of contribution to the world.

In fact, every successful business defines its definiteness of purpose by the problem it solves or the need that it serves. It is the mission of the business. As an individual you should also incorporate your personal mission statement that allows you to stay focused your definiteness of purpose.

The next step is Mastery over Self which is creating the self-discipline that creates positive habits that allow you to keep focused and demonstrates that you truly are in control of your thoughts and actions.

But in his wisdom, Hill also recognized that we all make mistakes, so we need to acknowledge them and learn from them. Too often when we make mistakes, instead of learning from them, we carry them around with us like heavy baggage defining ourselves as failures. It is important to understand that mistakes happen to all of us and when they do it is important to ask yourself what the lesson is...so you don't repeat the mistake. *It is important to remember that mistakes are occurrences...not definitions.*

But Hill also recognized that even the strongest faith can be tested by everyday life. He shared the importance of controlling our environment. What are you listening to? What are you reading? Who are you spending time with? Who are you listening to? Just imagine entering a room that is full of people crying at the funeral of a child...do you feel the emotional pull of sadness? Now imagine entering a room of people singing and dancing...where you immediately smile and feel the beat of the music. That small example demonstrates the impact of our environment on our attitude and emotional well-being.

It is very important to surround yourself with people who support you and want you to succeed. And it is even more important to limit your exposure to people who try to hold you back or pull you down. Environment includes what you and those around you feed your subconscious. In *Think and Grow Rich*, Hill shares the importance of Autosuggestion, feeding your mind and subconscious with positive messaging to bolster your outlook, your confidence and faith in yourself. It not only helps nurture your faith but gives you energy and motivation to move forward toward accomplishing your definiteness of purpose. When the pandemic stopped us in our tracks, I was distressed by all the negative messaging and the amount of fear and hopelessness it was generating. I took action and started sharing a daily message of hope and positivity, called daily ATMs (Abundance, Tips and Mentorship). The ATMs are an autosuggestion tool for you if you are looking for positive messaging and environment. I end each message every day with the same exercise. I ask you to repeat in the mirror, "I am fabulous!" And then I respond, "Yes you are!" (*atm.sharonlechter.com*)

Going hand in hand with controlling your environment, and equally as important is controlling your time. So often we know what we need to do…we just don't do it! (Are you feeling busted right now?) It could be fear that is holding you back or a lack of motivation. Start by analyzing your calendar. Are you spending time…or are you investing time? You can make money, lose it, and make it back. But time is your only truly precious resource. Once it is gone…you don't get it back. Commit to investing your time in the pursuit of your Definiteness of Purpose and you will feel the faith and confidence in yourself grow.

When I start working with new clients, I carefully review the Personal Success Equation with them. Entrepreneurship can be very lonely because entrepreneurs are trying to do everything themselves relying solely on their own passion and talent. This comes from being taught to work alone in school. But business is a team sport and collaboration is essential for innovation and success. While my clients are strong in their passion and talents, the areas that are often weakest for them in their Personal Success Equations are usually the Associations they have as well as the lack of Faith in themselves.

After years of mentoring clients, I can honestly say having the right Associations are the best and quickest way to build your Faith and confidence in yourself. Those new associations can include having the right mentor, people on your team who are strong where you are weak, the right advisors, and the right industry collaborators. When you have the right people around you and you have a bad day, they step up to bolster you and keep you focused on the big picture. They help transform your fear into faith. Having the team moving together toward your definiteness of purpose is much more fun and rewarding that trying to do it all alone.

To ensure you truly succeed and overcome any obstacles that may stand in your way, you definitely need the right association and faith. Having faith in yourself, your mission and your ability to succeed, will help you persevere when times are difficult and propel you to even greater heights of success.

When I wrote *Think and Grow Rich for Women*, I asked Sara O'Meara and Yvonne Fedderson to share their thoughts on Faith and I was so impressed with what they shared that I am including it here as well. Sara and Yvonne are the founders of Childhelp, the largest non-profit dedicated to the prevention and treatment of child abuse saving over 11 million children from the horrors of abuse. (www.childhelp.org) They have been nominated for the Nobel Peace Prize ten times. They are dear friends, mentors of mine, and true angels on earth. Here is some of what they shared:

THE FAITH TREE: GROWING, SURVIVING AND THRIVING GROWING

Money doesn't grow on trees, but faith does. Worry is interest paid on trouble before it is due, but Faith is like money in the bank.

Napoleon Hill wrote, "Faith is the starting point of all accumulation of riches." We often find we are where we choose to be. Faith gives us the courage to make necessary changes in our lives and allows us to grow in a clear and positive manner. Every dream shaped into a goal begins with the faith that if we plant a seed of hope, tend our garden with care and survive the storms that are sure to come our way, a thriving success will bloom.

When we began building our nonprofit, Childhelp, faith was the foundation; it became the soil in which we planted each advocacy center, residential treatment facility, hotline, adoption agency, foster care and group home. Soon we saw the fruits of our labor branching into national legislation and flowering into prevention education. We knew that advocating for abused children was part of God's plan and we would be guided through each season. We worked hard in the field every day but never doubted that a Higher Power was enriching our soil, nourishing our vision and ensuring the sun shone on our children.

But what if you have no faith? What if difficult times and disappointment leave you lacking the belief that you can be successful? The good news is that you can grow and know that you are growing. You can become stronger in faith, more knowledgeable in spirit and see it in yourself. A popular biblical parable posits that the smallest grain of faith, as miniscule as a mustard seed, can uproot trees and move mountains. Before you plant your tree, define successful growth and determine what will make your soil "rich."

When you choose to live your life in faith, desires and hopes will magnetize to you and you will begin to rise above the clouds. You will see beyond all seeming limitations and value yourself and others more. So ask yourself: Are you solely seeking monetary wealth or the richness of spirit that comes from being in the service of others?

SURVIVING

After the devastating attacks on America on September 11, 2001, a scorched tree with broken branches was discovered in the rubble at Ground Zero. It was a small Callery pear tree that had managed to sprout a few leaves beneath the destruction. Its discovery rejuvenated the spirits of weary rescue workers and became a symbol of recovery. They were determined to keep the tree alive and worked with local parks & recreation professionals to plant it at the site where so much had been lost. Even when a terrible storm uprooted it, the tree was replanted and once again flowered with white blossoms of hope. It was named "The Survivor Tree."

Children who have been abused and neglected come to us with their spirits scorched and their lives uprooted. At each Childhelp Residential Treatment Village, there is a garden where the little boys and girls in our care nurture fruits and vegetables from seed to plate, learning the cycle of growth but embodying the importance of survival. We teach that there is no challenge of the past that can stop the fulfillment of a fruitful future. Like "The Survivor Tree", they learn that a small seed can create something great that may be uprooted time and time again but always has the chance to branch out and become whole.

What if your past is blocking your progress or you keep experiencing setbacks? There is no need to look back except to acknowledge the lessons you have learned, taking only the positive from these experiences to draw upon in your future. Sorrow looks back, worry looks around and faith looks up. Napoleon Hill asserts, "Faith is the only known antidote to failure" and 2 Corinthians 4:13-18 promises, "Though outwardly we are wasting away, yet inwardly we are being renewed day by day. Four our light and momentary troubles are achieving for us eternal glory that far outweighs them all. So we fix our eyes not on what is seen, but what is unseen. For what is seen is temporary, but what is unseen is eternal." When you release your struggle to a Higher Power, you not only survive, you plant roots that will keep you strong forever.

THRIVING

Once you have grown in trust and survived the tests of your faith, you will enter a period of great power and responsibility. You will be victorious over your environment, weaknesses and all obstacles in your life when you follow God's path. This is your time to thrive! You have become confident in overcoming struggles and watched your dreams manifest. Suddenly, you can see the way in which a bright idea becomes a concrete reality. This is the final plateau of faith that Napoleon Hill so deftly defines, "Faith is the 'eternal elixir' which gives life, power, and action to the impulse of thought."

It is important to live and do your work in such a way that when others see you, their evaluation is the evidence of Faith. When that happens, you reap the rewards you rightfully deserve. One of the most important lessons we have learned is that success is not an endpoint and our thoughts shape each and every day. Our thoughts are our actions so positive thinking begets positive results. What's another word for positive thinking? Faith.

Matthew 12:33-37 speaks about using success responsibly, "The good person out of his good treasure brings forth good, and the evil person out of his evil treasure brings forth evil." The verse sums up perfectly, "Either make the tree good and its fruit good, or make the tree bad and its fruit bad, for the tree is known by its fruit." Thriving, then, is not just about how high you grow, it is ensuring that your branches never sprout poison bitter blossoms but rather that your fruit is always healthy and sweet.

Sara and Yvonne's Faith Tree certainly shows the depth of their giving natures, as well as their FAITH in each and every one of us. Let's review just a couple of their thoughts followed by how we can apply them to ourselves:

"Every dream shaped into a goal begins with the faith that if we plant a seed of hope, tend our garden with care and survive the storms that are sure to come our way, a thriving success will bloom."

Your definiteness of purpose (goal) when nurtured with action and faith will overcome obstacles and create the success you deserve.

"We worked hard in the field every day but never doubted that a Higher Power was enriching our soil, nourishing our vision and ensuring the sun shone on our children."

Work hard every day but never doubt that a higher power is enriching your soil, nourishing your vision and ensuring that the sun will shine on your endeavors.

If you are struggling to find ways to cultivate your own garden of faith, review the passage from Napoleon Hill and begin to harvest confidence in yourself.

SELF-CONFIDENCE FORMULA

Resolve to throw off the influences of any unfortunate environment, and to build your own life to ORDER. Taking inventory of mental assets and liabilities, you will discover that your greatest weakness is lack of self-confidence. This handicap can be surmounted, and timidity translated into courage, through the aid of auto-suggestion. The application of this principle may be made through a simple arrangement of positive thought impulses stated in writing, memorized, and repeated, until they become a part of the working equipment of the subconscious faculty of your mind.

First. I know that I have the ability to achieve the object of my Definite Purpose in life; therefore, I DEMAND of myself persistent, continuous action toward its attainment, and I here and now promise to render such action.

Second. I realize the dominating thoughts of my mind will eventually reproduce themselves in outward, physical action, and gradually transform themselves into physical reality; therefore, I will concentrate my thoughts, for thirty minutes daily, upon the task of thinking of the person I intend to become, thereby creating in my mind a clear mental picture.

Third. I know through the principle of auto-suggestion, any desire that I persistently hold in my mind will eventually seek expression through some practical means of attaining the object back of it, therefore, I will devote ten minutes dialing to demanding of myself the development of SELF-CONFIDENCE.

Fourth. I have clearly written down a description of my DEFINITE CHIEF AIM in life, and I will never stop trying until I shall have developed sufficient self-confidence for its attainment.

Fifth. I fully realize that no wealth or position can long endure, unless built on truth and justice; therefore, I will engage in no transaction which does not benefit all whom it affects. I will succeed by attracting to myself the forces I wish to use, and the cooperation of other people. I will induce others to serve me, because of my willingness to serve others. I will eliminate hatred, envy, jealously, selfishness, and cynicism, by developing love for all humanity, because I know that a negative attitude towards others can never bring me success. I will cause others to believe in me, because I will believe in them, and in myself.
I will sign my name to this formula, commit it to memory, and repeat it aloud once a day, with full FAITH that it will gradually influence my THOUGHTS and ACTIONS so that I will become a self-reliant and successful person."

As I end this chapter on Faith, I want to share how I acknowledge and request support from a higher power. I have strong faith in God and believe in his abundant love. My faith was dramatically tested in December of 2012 when my youngest son died. We are not supposed to outlive our children. My life went into neutral, or into the land of numb, for several years. In fact, I almost retired because I was unable to find the joy in life. It was the people around me that challenged me, and yes, I believe my son even whispered in my ear, "Get over it Mom…you are still here for a reason. There is more for you to do." At the same time someone sent me the book, *The Prayer of Jabez* by Bruce Wilkinson.

The Prayer of Jabez is a simple 4 line prayer found in the Old Testament 1 Chronicles 4: 9-10 that reads:

> **'Oh, that You would bless me indeed, and enlarge my territory, that Your hand would be with me, and that You would keep me from evil, that I may not cause pain.'**

This prayer has brought me great peace and faith. I say it every day and before every interview or speech so that I may add the greatest value each and every time. Below I share how each line impacts me each time I say it.

Oh, that you would bless me indeed – Dear God, thank you for blessing me with this opportunity.

Enlarge my territory – Allow me to reach a larger audience than I can imagine.

Your hand would be with me – Use me as your vessel and help me deliver the right message for the people before me.

Keep me from evil, that I may not cause pain – Help me make sure the message is a force for good and adding value.

In closing, I want to remind you that you are FABULOUS! No matter what you have been through, or what may have stopped you in your tracks…you are still here for a reason! And you can help others going through what you have survived. Have faith in yourself and use that faith to help others find the faith in themselves. And then ask yourself.

Have you added value to someone's life today?

I have faith in you!

~ **Sharon Lechter**

Author of *Think and Grow Rich for Women*, Co-author of *Exit Rich, Three Feet From Gold, Outwitting the Devil, Success and Something Greater, The 13 Steps to Riches, Rich Dad Poor Dad* and 14 other Rich Dad books.

SHARON LECHTER

As an Entrepreneur, International Speaker, Bestselling Author, Mentor, Philanthropist, Licensed CPA for 35 years, and a Chartered Global Management Accountant, Sharon Lechter is the premier expert for financial literacy and entrepreneurial success. A lifelong education advocate, in 1989, Sharon joined forces with the inventor of the first electronic 'talking book' and helped him expand the electronic book industry to a multi-million dollar international market.

In 1997 Sharon co-authored the international bestseller *Rich Dad Poor Dad* and has released 14 other books in the Rich Dad series. Over 10 years as the co-founder and CEO, she built the empire into the world's leading personal finance brand.

In 2008, she was asked by the Napoleon Hill Foundation to help re-energize the powerful teachings of Napoleon Hill just as the international economy was faltering. Sharon has released four bestselling books in cooperation with the Foundation, including *Think and Grow Rich*, *Three Feet from Gold*, *Outwitting the Devil*, *Think and Grow Rich for Women*, and *Success and Something Greater..* She is also featured in the 2017 movie *Think and Grow Rich: The Legacy.* Her most recent books include *Exit Rich* in cooperation with INC Magazine and *How Money Works for Women with Wealthwave Media LLC..*

Sharon is a highly sought-after mentor and has worked with major brands like Disney and Time Warner and served two U.S. Presidents as an advisor on the topic of financial literacy. As CEO of Pay Your Family First, she has dedicated her entrepreneurial efforts to the creation and distribution of financial education books, games, curriculums, and other experiential learning projects. Everything about Sharon's career centers around impacting others to improve their financial IQ, access untapped potential personally and in business, and create their own legacy.

But everything changed in 2012 when Sharon's son unexpectedly died. All of Sharon's successes seemed to fade into the background. She kept working but on autopilot. She stopped playing at the level she always had and was living in neutral for a couple of years.

In 2014, Sharon decided to REFIRE instead of Retire and to play big again, and she wants you to as well with the Play Big Movement. It's time to shed the limitations that have stopped you in the past. It's time to play big, master your money and time and create maximum impact.

Sharon lives in Scottsdale, AZ, with her husband and business partner, Michael Lechter, a powerhouse in the area of Intellectual Property, Organizational Architecture, and Publishing. Together, they love spending time with each other and especially like to get away to their dude ranch, Cherry Creek Lodge (*www.cherrycreeklodge.com*), where they can get "off the grid" (literally) and get recharged for their next big play.

Sharon continues to be a committed philanthropist by giving back to world communities both as a benefactor and a volunteer and has been honored with numerous awards.

CHAPTER 3

EVERYDAY MIRACLES

"You have not because you ask not."
~ James 4:2-3

I believe in miracles. Do you?

Throughout the end of my forties and into my next decade of life, I experienced a huge range of trauma and health challenges. The lifestyle changes my family and I endured during this time seem remarkable as I reflect back onto what has become our normal.

In 2014, I was involved in an automobile accident that shifted my life and set me on a rollercoaster ride I never anticipated. I was plummeted into a life of silence and the inability to walk without assistance for two years. Those years felt like a few months to me because, unbeknownst to my family and me, I had obtained a traumatic brain injury (TBI) to four parts of my brain. These injuries left me completely cognizant of what was happening and spoken around me, without the ability to react or communicate. I was trapped within my mind.

Have you ever been alone with your thoughts? It seems as if all your inner critics come out to play and stir up insecurities about love, worthiness, and capability. That is what occurred with me. I battled daily with my inner critics. At first, I agreed with them. I fell into the "woe is me" trap. Maybe I was left in this state because I had no life plan? Perhaps my voice was taken away because I had nothing to contribute? Maybe I became helpless because I squandered my days with worry and lived so stuck in my ruts that there was no time for play?

In my head, I berated myself for not having a plan, not enjoying the simplicity of what life has to offer, and my most guilty habit of being stuck in a rut and expecting the world to adjust to make my dreams come true. I felt unproductive, lazy, stupid, worthless, a burden, and careless to have allowed myself to be in an auto accident.

Somewhere in my journey of being isolated with my thoughts, I realized that I was becoming less aware. I felt my mind slipping away. My health was also slipping. I would become dizzy and my headaches were more severe. My family would say comments that they didn't think I understood, regarding my response time to stimuli. I became very depressed. I preferred death over continuing to live in this state.

Somewhere near the end of the two years of being completely helpless, I was very frustrated. I was placed on the loveseat in our living room, just as I had been placed for the past seven hundred and thirty days. I would sit there until my husband came home to move me. The thoughts of being useless flooded my mind. I made plans to take my life. The irony was tha I was unable to move in order to orchestrate the plan. I was furious! I screamed inside of my mind, "If you hate me so much, kill me already!" While tears streamed down my face, I heard a booming voice say, "You're not dead, yet! Get up!" Some may think that voice was a figment of my imagination; I know it wasn't. The moment I heard the voice, I saw a high speed movie reel of my life. Each point that I thought I was alone and left for dead, there was some unseen being with me. I knew that I would actually be dead if I wasn't being protected. I found myself several feet away from the loveseat I had become accustomed to, on my knees thanking God for all I had endured during my life.

There was another thought that came to me which brought a sense of peace, "I have never been alone." I thanked God for every trial I had experienced, because it prepared me for the next. I promised to no longer question the "why" behind my experiences and to seek gratitude in every day. I asked to be able to speak again so I could share what I learned with others —that life is precious and each of us is worthy of living as our best selves every day.

My recovery from my TBI has been long. I didn't get up and start walking and talking immediately, it took work. I had to train myself out of my old habits of berating myself. I found that there is power in our words. Remember when I told you about my decline in health and reaction time I experienced when stuck in my head? There was no physical cause for it. I convinced my mind, by berating myself over and over again, that I was not worthy of healing. I inadvertently created negative affirmations of being unproductive, lazy, stupid, worthless, a burden, and careless so well, that my body responded.

I knew I needed to restructure my mindset. I found guidance in my mentor, Dr. Paul Scheele. He once said that humans are built to be resilient. Look at a baby learning to walk, "They get up, they fall. They get up, they fall." If babies had the mindset of adults, we would be a "world of crawlers." If words have power, I needed to learn how to take control of how I used those words in my life to heal myself. I needed to rediscover my toddler mindset to believe in myself. It took deep inner work to accomplish this task. My daily mantra in my head revolved around my complete healing or better. I used my imagination to see, feel, taste, and embody how I would be as the newly improved me. I believed that this reality existed; it was simply awaiting me to catch up to it. Every morning before I opened my eyes and every night as I closed my eyes, I would see the me I wanted to be. I knew how it felt to be in my healed body. I became the me I am today within my mind, years before I arrived. Now, I am known for my positive attitude. As a matter of fact, I was recognized by the John Maxwell Team with the Culture Award for that very attribute.

Whether or not you believe in God is your business. I don't consider myself an overly religious person. I simply share what I experienced. My words have power, which means everyone's words have power. I've seen it in action up-close and personal. You have, too! How often have you said to yourself, or even just joking with another person, "I'm always broke. I have horrible luck dating. I won't get that raise. There are no more good men/women in the world. I'll never (fill in the blank)." This negative or self-depreciation talk is a form of Auto Suggestion. We say these words like they just go into the wind without effect, but the emotional ground from which we proclaim those attributes give the words power and in turn, becomes our reality.

"In the beginning was the Word, and the Word was with God, and the Word was God."
~ John 1, NKJ

Earlier, I asked if you believe in miracles. If my story didn't provide enough proof, I challenge you to look for them throughout your days. Miracles occur right before our eyes, but we are too consumed with how much we aren't deserving that we don't recognize the gifts that fall before us, perhaps because they don't reveal themselves in the ways we want them to be presented. Observe the intricacies of a leaf. Watch a bee buzz from flower to flower. Ponder the magnitude of the sky above us and how the clouds move. I ask that you do an experiment with the words you say outwardly and to yourself when no one else is around. Focus on one statement you have been guilty of saying and flip it into a positive statement. Use only uplifting language, like, "I am worthy of (fill in the blank)." Believe it. Live as if it is already in your life. Use as many senses you can muster to feel the sensation of whatever you are worthy of and how you feel once you have it. See the miracles begin to be more evident.

I believe in miracles, big and small. Not because I recovered from my TBI, but rather that I obtained my TBI in the first place. It was a harsh wake-up call in order to live with purpose. I had to lose myself to find the willpower to seek what I wanted out of life. I became intentional with my thoughts and actions. I used to live my life feeling inadequate and powerless. The miracle is that through the rollercoaster ride, I learned to love, accept, and honor myself to be the best version of me every day and to be so—unapologetically!

SELF-LEADERSHIP

Napoleon Hill's Concept On "Auto Suggestion"

Self-Leadership is:

"How to Get Yourself to Do What Needs to be Done, When it Needs to be Done, Whether You Feel Like it Yet or Not."

It is how you mold the world around you and within you to assist toward your goal to live an abundant and rewarding life.

In Chapter 4 of *Think and Grow Rich*, author Napoleon Hill calls this, "The Medium for Influencing the Subconscious Mind. The Third Step toward Riches."

This is about "ALL suggestions and all self-administered stimuli which reach one's mind through the five senses." This applies to what you permit as well as what you choose. The conscious mind is your gatekeeper for what enters your subconscious mind.

Hill recommends:

Read your written desire aloud twice daily and see and *feel* yourself already in possession of what you want.

Faith is the activator; you must *feel* the reward you seek.

Reading the words is useless unless you *feel* the reward.

You must mentally and emotionally *experience* the payoff you seek.

If you don't believe it consciously, then your subconscious won't believe it either.

Faith is the new skill you must learn to master.

We've all heard, "You've got to believe in yourself." Yes, that's nice to say, but how does one do it? The how—that is the master key to riches. Auto Suggestion is how you get there.

I've taught for decades that success must be M.A.D.E.

M - We need a clear Mental Image of what we want.

A - We need to live Affirmations of all types to reinforce our belief.

D - We need Daily Successes to give us real-world success experiences of all types.

E - We need Environmental Influences that grow our belief.

All of these are within your reach.

Wisdom and cleverness cannot shorten the path to success; they simply make parts of it more efficient. You must persist in this until the goal is reached. That's the price. No freebies are possible. Be exact and concentrate until you *feel* what you see. From this daily practice will come the Burning Desire that compels you toward your goal.

Assume the outcome is inevitable if you keep your "magnet" activated. Your magnet is the visual image and the resulting burning desire of what you want. Allow it to turn off and all the other forces of the universe will draw things toward them instead of toward you. Starting over may take you longer. Keep this practice in place daily.

Let the universe bring you what you seek. You must attract it through your mindset and actions. There is enough for everyone in the universe. There always was and always will be.

Your subconscious will reveal the practical plan to get your desire. Don't wait to have a plan, *experience* the payoff in your mind and heart daily now! Expect it!

When the plan arrives, act immediately! See yourself doing the work or service for which you will be paid. Close your eyes and practice this until it is compelling to you. Daily, daily, daily, daily— did I say daily?

Become the person who will attract the future you desire.

Acquire all the traits, habits, and characteristics that will make you the obvious go-to person for the opportunities you want.

J. Paul Getty once wrote a book titled *How to Be Rich*. Note the emphasis, not how to Get rich but rather how to Be rich. Many sad stories exist about poor people who won the lottery yet couldn't keep the riches. They had poor-person habits and thinking. They acquired millions of dollars with no effort and then they squandered it with bad choices. If you don't change your thinking, then any improvement in your circumstances will only be temporary.

MENTAL IMAGE

I remember when I was a $525 a month clerk at the housing authority dreaming of future success. One day I fantasized about winning millions in the lottery. But rather than listing all the luxuries and indulgences I'd buy, I wrote out a plan for financially securing my entire lifetime and my family's as well.

On paper, I created a charitable foundation and a set of rules for selecting the family members who would serve on the board of trustees. The service was in a two-year rotation between members of my extended family so that everyone had a chance to participate but nobody could dominate. I made a set of rules that started with, "Any person who is caught lying or acting in a selfish or deceptive way related to this foundation will not only lose their position on the board, but they will be excluded from the benefits of this foundation forever and so will their immediate family members."

With advice from friends and people whom I admired, I crafted a set of rules for the foundation that would assure its survival long into the future and would allow every family member to benefit in meaningful ways from the money. No debt bailouts for spendthrifts, no special gifts for certain people, just financial security, and disaster-relief for all of us.

I never did win the lottery, nor did I create that foundation, but the thinking and preparation I did over those many months laid a foundation for my entire career. Yes, I did go on to earn millions of dollars and to achieve worldwide recognition in my field of motivation and human development. And for all these 40+ years, I've operated with a sound financial foundation.

The vision of what you want is your bedrock. That is what you create your Mental Image from. Then as you clarify the picture in your mind, the steps to make it a reality will come to you. Write them down and take action. Make it real in any way that you can.
Create a vision board or poster with images of what you want your life to be like. Make a folder in your phone of photos and images that give you the feelings you are seeking. Improve it constantly until it is perfect and review it often.

You cannot cheat your way to success. You can deceive others and gain temporary wins, but you'll become a crook. You won't respect yourself, nor will others. Bernie Madoff and other famous swindlers may have lived the high life for a while, but payment must always come.

Learn a new language, the language of success. Your words shape your mind, and your mind selects your actions. So watch your thoughts with care. Let me give you a few examples of how our words affirm either what we want or what we don't.

- When you say you can't, your mind hears it too. Our chosen words are interpreted by our subconscious mind as directions. It doesn't judge, it just follows and facilitates what it is fed.

If you MUST say "can't", then at least add "yet." Make your limitations temporary, not permanent.

- How do you talk about yourself? What labels have you adopted to describe yourself?

Do you say, "I'm the middle child," "I'm the runt of the litter," "I've never been good at math," "I just don't seem to be very (insert a category: creative, strong, sensitive, etc.," "I don't care about money or prestige, I just want a good life," "I've never been able to keep weight off," "I have big bones or slow metabolism," "You never know when things might go wrong." (Yes, you do.) "You can never be too careful." (Of course, you can!)

All of these are messages to your subconscious as to what to expect from yourself. Most are excuses for not living up to your potential. They are rationalizations that are designed to help you feel OK about being broke, left out, not proud of yourself, etc.

How about something as simple as "I can't remember"? How do you know you "can't"? When did you give up trying? Instead, say, "I don't remember yet." That's the truth, and it doesn't limit you from remembering. "I can't" means it cannot happen. "I don't" means that at present it hasn't happened yet.

- Refuse to criticize others. Don't buy into the soap-opera mentality that life is awful and then you die. Soap-opera TV shows feed on loneliness and fear. They cultivate the belief that nobody can be trusted, all will betray you, nobody is what they seem, and life is about greed, power, and sex. Stop it! Don't go there. Guard your mind and your language. Go toward the Light!

- Cold Calls – In selling, the action of making new calls on people you don't know is a critical element in success. Nobody succeeds by only calling on the people they already know unless they know thousands of them. And, if you wait for them to call you or to expect your call, you will have a lifelong wait. So, businesses encourage what is known as "cold calls."

Why cold? They say it is because the people don't expect to hear from you.

I challenge that. If they don't expect you, or you haven't called on them before, then why not use a term that describes the actual event? Call them what they are "New calls." Not "warm calls," that's just too juvenile. Besides, calls don't have a temperature. They are either new calls or subsequent calls.

So what? Well, if you make it a cold call in your mind then you will react accordingly. You'll feel unwelcome, like an intruder, and you'll be on the defensive from the start. You will be trying to justify the call. If it is simply a new call, then you can focus on your purpose: to find people you can help by selling your product or service.

- Here's another sales term that doesn't work: Closing.

"What?" you ask. "Surely you know that I must ask for the order if I'm to get the sale!"

True, but you don't have to close anything to do it.

"Close" means to shut, to end, terminate, discontinue, or finalize. We say, "the case is closed," this is a "closed market", she had a "closed mind", or "Sorry, we are closed. Come back tomorrow." All of these are acts that end or shut out something.

In sales, we want to earn a profit by helping our customer. That means we are forming a new business friendship, not a social one, but one based on mutual financial benefit.

You ask, "Do you mean that I should call it 'Opening' the sale?" No, of course not. But call it what it is: Confirming the purchase. You confirm a sale, you don't end it. A confirmation is the action that makes a purchase official.

Once the sale is confirmed, you begin a new relationship in which you provide benefits to the buyer and they provide payment to you. Nothing closed about it. In fact, you probably want it to lead to a lifetime of purchases and referrals.

Record yourself saying (with feeling!) what you want to become real. Say it like you mean it or don't say it at all. Treat this affirmation as you would treat an apology. Saying the words doesn't count unless the person hearing it believes that you mean it. Listen to yourself saying it, describing what it will be like, feeling the result.

Keep this in mind: whatever you say, you hear it too! Your mind accommodates what your words imply. "I hate selling. I just want to help people." That's the voice of fear speaking. That is self-doubt on display. The implication is that either selling is a bad thing, or you don't believe in your offer strongly enough to overcome reluctance to buy it. Can you truly help people? If what you offer is really worth considering, then why wouldn't you want people to consider it?

DAILY SUCCESSES

When I was in the Army, I went through Basic Combat Training. Everything we did was part of a process to make us more effective in armed combat situations. We learned to obey orders from our leaders without hesitation and without challenge. We learned to jump out of bed at the sound of Reveille. We learned to march in formation so well that we acted as one body of men, not separate individuals. Everything counted because, in combat, our lives and other lives were at stake.

In Officers Candidate School, the same discipline was in place. How we made our beds, arranged our uniforms in the closet, shined our shoes, cleaned our weapons, saluted others all counted. Everything counted! We became highly aware of little details and very disciplined about doing what mattered, even the smallest things.

Daily life isn't military service for most of us, but the discipline and confidence that comes from achieving Minimum Daily Standards should be important to all of us. If you don't make your bed each morning, clean up after yourself, wash the dishes instead of leaving them in the sink, keep your personal grooming good and cleanliness excellent, then you will lose respect for yourself. Each small negligence on your part is like a word of discouragement from someone you respect.

Conversely, each small success helps build your confidence bank account and self-respect.

Find something in each key category of your life that you can achieve no matter what else happens that day. Feed your mind, exercise your reason, nurture your friendships, listen to your family members, exercise your body, observe your use of money, improve your work, practice your faith, explore great ideas, and have some fun! Whichever part of life you neglect will sooner or later interrupt the other parts to gain your attention. If you neglect fitness, then you will be forced to make time for illness, etc.

Do ONE thing in each area, no matter how small. If you want to become a runner, put on your running shoes every day and step outside. You don't have to run, but you must form the habit of showing up prepared to run. Once you master the micro-moves, discipline is within your reach.

Keep a record of every dollar you receive and spend. Keep it where you will see it. Become money-conscious and you'll begin to manage money better.

Spend 5 minutes in direct conversation with each immediate family member every day. Not incidental conversation but intentional listening and talking. Spend longer when you can.

Reach out to one friend every day and just ask how they are or tell them that you were thinking about them.

Contribute one better idea each day to your work. Share your improvements with others, but don't expect them to adopt them. Just share them.

Read one passage in the Bible or your faith text each day. Thank God for your blessings and list them each night when you go to bed.

Learn one thing today that you wouldn't have learned without trying.

Do a word puzzle or Sudoku math exercise or solve a problem today.

ENVIRONMENTAL INFLUENCES

Look around you. What do you see? How does it make you feel? Encouraged or not?

Control what you can, adapt to what you cannot change.
You can structure your surroundings to be your helper. To clarify your Mental Image, go and sample what you dream of. Have lunch at a five-star hotel, test drive your dream car, take a snack and sit by the lake where you want to live. Rent a boat for the weekend or the day.

Go to the concert or club where you someday want to perform. Stand on the stage in the convention center or showroom where you will give a speech or receive an award. Buy a poster, or get a fold-out sales brochure, or a scale model of what you want. See yourself owning or using these each day.

Shop for the clothes you hope to afford, sit on the furniture you plan to buy someday. You don't need to go into debt, just get a feel for the items. Put yourself into the picture.

Get around people who share your enthusiasm and drastically reduce the time you spend around pessimists, doubters, and sourpusses. Don't participate in pity parties or criticism and bashing of others. Avoid political debates while you are seeking to succeed.

Choose the movies you watch with your goal as your filter. Don't go to occult or tragic or hateful or victim movies. Read uplifting novels, true stories, auto biographies, heroic, and inspiring works. Listen to positive podcasts, radio shows, webinars, and read blogs that lift you up. Manage your environment, don't let it manage you.

Create a vision board of images, a photo file, a playlist, slogans, tokens, symbols, and metaphors that make your goal more real. Start now to intentionally experience the success you dream about. Make it real, *feel* it.

Here is my personal story:

When I was in my twenties, I never expected to have a life that mattered much. My expectations were that I would get a middle-management office job at the phone company (where my Dad worked as a repairman) and retire at 65, then die whenever the statistics for my age group were up. I didn't have a college degree; nobody I knew had money and no one was encouraging me to achieve big things. My family loved me but didn't actively encourage reading, critical thinking, or aspiring to excellence or success.

One day, after hearing an inspiring message from Earl Nightingale on the radio, I started dreaming bigger. While working as an entry-level clerk in a government agency in

Little Rock, Arkansas, I got a course catalog from the University of Arkansas at Little Rock and started listing the courses I would like to attend. There were more than 30 diverse courses that I found interesting, yet I still didn't know what I wanted as my career. I took a couple of night courses but didn't re-enroll.

Soon, I began to read motivational books and listen to recordings. There weren't many at the time, this was in 1972. I read *Think and Grow Rich* by Napoleon Hill, *The Power of Positive Thinking* by Norman Vincent Peale, and *How to Win Friends and Influence People* by Dale Carnegie. I listened to *The Strangest Secret* by Earl Nightingale and many recordings from Success Motivation Institute and Paul J. Meyer. Then it hit me! I want to do what these people do! I want to work in motivational training and be a speaker like Hill, Nightingale, Peale, and Carnegie.

But I had two limitations: I had never given a public speech and I had nothing worthwhile to say. That's a big limit! So, I started following the advice in each of their books. I set goals: lifetime goals, 5-year goals, 1-year goals, and daily actions to take. I wrote down my dreams and wishes. I clipped photos from magazines and pasted them where I would see them daily.

I changed my circle of friends by including people who also wanted to achieve great things and reduced the amount of time I spent with people who were pessimistic or small-minded. I disciplined myself to use optimistic language and stopped running myself down. I began a discipline of doing at least one good thing in each area of my life daily. There were positive statements and goal descriptions on my bathroom mirror, the visor of my car, and in my notebook. Every day, I listened to motivational recordings… every day.

This continued for five years.

In the first three years of this life change, I went from being a clerk to being the staff assistant to the Board of Directors in the agency where I worked. I was elected president of our employee's association. I joined the Jaycees (Junior Chamber of Commerce) and became very actively involved in volunteer work. At the office, I got a raise, then a promotion and another raise.

One day, a man named Harold Gash came to me after a Jaycees meeting where he and I were both giving presentations. He said, "Jim, you have more potential than any young man I have ever known! You should come to work with me and sell Earl Nightingale's motivational recordings to businesses." I was aghast! Me? Sell? "But I'm not good at selling," I said.

Harold said, "Yes, Jim, you can be an excellent salesman. But first you need to change your thinking." He was right. I had the ability, just not the mindset I needed.

Over the ensuing months, I left the government job and worked full-time with Harold. As I listened to the recordings daily and made calls to tell others about them, I made sales. In fact, I did well and loved the work! Then the US Jaycees national headquarters called me and asked if I would apply for the job of Individual Development Senior Program Manager for the 356,000 members of the Jaycees.

On September 1, 1975, I went to work at the Jaycees HQ in Tulsa, Oklahoma. I was a full-time trainer and speaker in the field of human development, just like my dream goals had stated back in Little Rock in 1972. I flew all over the country and gave speeches to groups as large as one thousand. I wrote training manuals and collaborated with leading experts like Og Mandino and W. Clement Stone (Look them up). I met Cavett Robert, founder of the National Speakers Association. My life profoundly changed.

While at the Jaycees HQ, I still listened to recordings daily, read books voraciously, and had written goals on cards in my bathroom, desktop, closet, and sun visor. I was living a daily regimen of Minimum Daily Standards of behavior that would achieve my goals. I started jogging and working out, lost 52 pounds of fat and became an amateur athlete... at age 30. My life transformed!

In June of 1977, I left the Jaycees and went full-time into professional speaking. Since that time, I have delivered over 3,300 paid speeches to millions of people, done three round-the-world lecture tours, delivered a TEDx talk that has more than 2,400,000 views, authored 20 books, including three international bestsellers, served as president of the National Speakers Association, and received every major award given to professional speakers in the world!

Earl Nightingale called me in 1984 after reading an article I had published, and he subsequently published my audio program, coauthored with Dr. Tony Alessandra, titled "Relationship Strategies for dealing with the differences in people." It sold more than $3.5 million dollars' worth in the first two years on the market! Note: In 1972, I heard him on the radio. In 1974, I was selling his recordings. In 1984, he was selling mine!

Over the years since then, I have become friends with Norman Vincent Peale, Og Mandino, Zig Ziglar, Dr. Denis Waitley, Tom Hopkins, Mark Victor Hansen, Jack Canfield, Brian Tracy, Les Brown, Don Hutson, Cavett Robert, Patricia Fripp, Jeanne Robertson, and many of the great names in human development. I've worked with W. Clement Stone and done *The Fire Walk Experience* with Tony Robbins. I've had my own TV Show on The Success Training Network, hosted a daily radio show, published hundreds of video lessons with Clay Clark, and lectured in 23 major cities across China to hundreds of thousands of people. My books have been published in multiple languages all around the world and I've written college textbooks. I'm a professor for the School of Management at California Lutheran University. And... I could go on, but surely, you get the point. All of this was achieved without outside funding, a government assistance program, a diversity grant or exception to "level the playing field" for me.

I had no college degree, no money to start with, no connections with successful people, no mentor nor encourager to get me started. I was out of shape, overweight by 52 pounds, and had no skills that I could quickly apply to get started. My job was a $525 a month clerkship at a local office of the housing authority. What I have done isn't important except for the fact that: If I can do this, YOU can do this!

Your success will be M.A.D.E. by you.

You already choose which Mental Images to accept. Your words affirm your current state of mind and circumstances. You have daily experiences that reinforce the world you've occupied up to now. Around you are environmental influences at every turn.

What I'm recommending is that you start making all of them INTENTIONAL.

Take charge of the influences in your life that are having Auto Suggestion impact on you every day. Make your life what you want it to be!

JIM CATHCART

Jim Cathcart, CSP, CPAE has achieved every professional speaker's dream: a Top 1% TEDx video, President of the National Speakers Association, Sales & Marketing Hall of Fame, Speakers Hall of Fame, The Golden Gavel Award, The Cavett Award, 21 published books, 3,300 paid speeches in all 50 states and 4 around-the-world lecture tours, and honored to be a Celebrity Featured Author in Erik "Mr. Awesome" Swanson's *The 13 Steps To Riches - Auto Suggestion #1* Bestselling book series! He is a University Executive MBA professor, and he has also been happily married for 51 years, remained trim and fit despite prostate cancer and a pacemaker in his 60s. He plays guitar and sings in nightclubs and is a life member of the American Motorcyclist Association. Someone said he is what "Fonzie" (from the TV show Happy Days) would be if he had gone to business school. Starting with nothing but dreams and willingness to earn his way, he can clearly show others how to become the person who will attract the future you want.

CHAPTER 4

RECALL. RETRIEVE. REUSE.

"Knowledge is power."
~ **School House Rock**

Have you ever witnessed a child being born? Before the birth, there are high levels of fear, anxiety, and chaos, intermixed with periods of such intense quiet among the high activity. So much so that the mother wonders, "Is my baby alright?" When the mother experiences unfathomable pain and wants to give up, that is the moment the new life makes the grand entrance. The prize comes after the painful experience.

This is when our foundation of Specialized Knowledge lessons begin. I believe we learn while in the womb. I remember my children responding and reacting to my activities, what I listened to, and what I ate while I carried them within me for nine months. Regardless, let's focus on the lessons we learn outside of the womb.

Imagine a newborn. Helpless, yes. Unaware, not so much. I view newborn babies as highly complex computers that rapidly acquire information with unlimited storage capabilities. When a baby takes its first breath, opens its eyes, and takes in the shocking changes of light, temperature, pressure, and security, it cries out in distress. Their little minds are computing the new stimuli and categorizing it. "What is going on?" "This is new!" "I am not comfortable!" "Put me back!" The baby does all this because it is removed from its comfort zone and becomes stressed. Sound familiar?

Most challenges you face as an adult have been seen or experienced on some level throughout your lifetime. As infants, we learn to distinguish sounds and smells. For instance, which voice feeds us, what they smell like, who doesn't feed us, and the different noises, i.e., doorbell, pets, music box, television, etc. We begin to learn this information within the first hours after birth. In every aspect of our developmental process, we are learning, adapting, and adjusting our programing. We have our highly complex computer brains acquiring information at a fast pace, processing and storing.

How often have you found yourself in a new situation, new job, a group of unfamiliar people, or something as simple as an elevator? The awkwardness is practically overwhelming. Why? We were taught at birth that anything outside of our normal (womb comfort zone) is scary.

The next set of tools we learn as we age are the skills around learning to use our muscles, pull up, stand, and eventually walk. Our super-computer brain now must collect all the information it gathered as we were born and has observed from our backs and bellies. The vast amount of data gathered, recalled, retrieved, and reused on a moment-to-moment basis is astronomical. Now, apply it to learning how to use these weird appendages. We grasp objects, faces, and eventually any solid object we can grip. We learn to move our legs under us to push up onto our hands and knees, and eventually manipulate them in sequence move to our bodies. We test the stability of objects near us to eventually pull up into a standing position and use the flexibility of our knees. We learn to bounce and test the strength and bend of our knees.

We move our feet to begin to walk while steadying ourselves on an object. Eventually, we let it go. We release what creates stability to venture into the unknown. We fall onto our knees, sometimes straight onto our faces. We cry in pain and frustration, but find a way to pull back up, hold our secure object for support, and again, release it to walk solo. Over and over again, we fall and get back up until one day, we walk without falling. Success! Our computer mind has now taken in thousands of data points, recalled variations, retrieved the best data for the task of getting up, walking, and reused it to keep us moving forward.

These basic Specialized Knowledge examples are fundamental to success. What helps you get up when another stays down? How do two people face similar life challenges and come out on the other side completely different; one more hopeful and the other full of doubt? Specialized Knowledge is the key to resilience and success. You owe it to yourself and society to discover your core skills not learned from an institution or formal training. Get back to your roots. That is where you will find the strength, willpower, and determination to be successful in whatever you choose to do.

We learned the core skills of success by surviving our first years of life:

1. Be cognizant of your surroundings.
2. Recognize who and what can be trusted.
3. Know when you feel unsafe.
4. Pursue your hunger/goals.
5. Reach up.
6. To reach your goal, sometime you will fall.
7. Falling hurts.
8. Getting back up is fulfilling.
9. Baby steps add up to great strides.
10. If you don't succeed, do it again with slight adjustments.

Change is not easy. Change is not butterflies in a field of daisies. It's scary. It's uncomfortable. The beauty of change is in the possibilities. This is the basis of much of my professional speaking and coaching material. My examples are derived from my life and the experiences shared by my clients. Unbeknownst to many, we each have vast knowledge stored within us. It's helpful to have a guide, mentor, or coach to guide the recall, retrieval, and reuse process to help us navigate through our challenges and toward our goals. Because, "We can't see the forest for the trees." - John Heywood

No one can do the mathematical calculations necessary to catch a baseball in real time. Yet, through years of practice and experience, a player can catch a ball moving at high velocity without performing the calculations. It is a perfect example of Specialized Knowledge.

Think of the major lessons you have learned throughout your life. What are they? My challenge to you is to list them out. Then, list all the less-significant lessons you learned in order to reach the major lesson. Those minor lessons are just as important as the major lessons. Take note of the minor lessons, because from those we can develop the foundation of resilience. The sub-data acquired is where the Specialized Knowledge building blocks lay. The importance of this sub list is immense because they are what we need to increase the success ratio when addressing a challenge. The ability to quickly adapt to recall, retrieve, and reuse old data is what sets you apart from the pack of others addressing the same issue. Remember, each of us has a unique processing code. This is our unique way of problem solving. This is the first of our Specialized Knowledge.

Throughout my travels in coaching, a common theme among the people I meet is that they are seeking something outside of themselves to reach the next level of success. All you need is inside your master computer. Learn how to access that knowledge, trust yourself, and be willing to fall. Multitudes of degrees, certifications, and the like are helpful for opening doors, but what actually lands the opportunity and secures the position is your personality: how you adapt to new environments, and your ability to learn new skills quickly. Where do those soft skills develop? Where do they stem from? Specialized Knowledge is how we recall, adapt, and reuse old information processed through our life experiences. This is how we are designed. Trust the toddler instinct within you, steady yourself, take that step, be ready to fall, and most importantly, get back up.

Just as a mother gives birth to a child, your ideas, goals, and breakthroughs in business and in life will come to fruition just beyond what you believe is your breaking point. Keep pushing through whatever seems to be in your way. Do it afraid. Being afraid means you care about the outcome. That's good! Complacency does not lead to success. Give your best efforts in all you do. Find your lessons. As long as you learn, you succeed.

Be the best version of you, unapologetically.

EXCERPT BY MICHAEL E. GERBER

WELCOME TO A SPECIAL NEW WORLD

It has been thought by those at the heart of our business universe that general knowledge is essential for a business' success. Meaning, knowing how to do all of the essential things a company is both created to do and, in the course of growing in its market, forced to do, whether to compete successfully with all the others attempting to secure a foothold in that world each has designs to successfully inhabit, or whether, even more hopefully, to wrest a leadership role in that marketplace by overcoming all other competitors' efforts at same.

It's the general knowledge that begs this conversation, the belief that knowing how to do everything "generally" will forge a truly competitive enterprise into a market leader. Or, if not that, at least make one out to be competitive.

So it is that a summary review of all companies within any market, no matter what the product or service, no matter what its intention is, no matter how much experience may be put into play, that summary will reveal a surprising to most of us, realization that in the main, each and every one of those companies, look, act and feel very much the same.

Oh, yes, their name is different. Ford is Ford. Chevrolet is Chevrolet. And so forth and so on.

But despite the apparent differences between a Ford Mustang and a Chevrolet Corvette, when you walk into their dealerships, or watch their advertising, or talk to one of their salespeople, or go into their service centers, what you'll find will be, without question, very much the same.

Indeed, it's the un-bewildering sameness of the world of companies on our planet which is an almost eerie repository of the un-bewildering sameness of all our people, no matter their race, no matter their sex, no matter their politics, no matter their insistence that they're indelibly unique, one and all, as original as the day they were born. Uniquely, Sam, Uniquely Alex, Uniquely Jezebel, uniquely their own.

Oh, if that were only true! What we find, unfortunately, is exactly the opposite. Glaringly opposite.

The extreme ordinariness of our paths, of our choices, of our employment, of our work, of our creativity, of our discipline, of our hopes and intentions, flails out at even the most casual observer, especially when we're engaged in the pursuit of the special in the world of our so-called entrepreneurs.

I say so-called entrepreneurs, because that resides at the heart of the matter, the heart of the absence of Specialized Knowledge.

The heart of the dissolute fact that the reality of Specialized Knowledge is that in the broad universe of commercial activity here in America and, even more distastefully, throughout the rest of the world, Specialized Knowledge is looked upon, if it's looked upon at all, as a foreign, unnecessary, foolish idea wresting for too much time, too much capital, and far too much insistence upon creativity than is necessary to do business at all.

In this book, *The 13 Steps To Riches - Volume 4 Specialized Knowledge*, we deal with that subject in a most specialized manner. We look upon Specialized Knowledge through the lens of a universal creator. A universally inspired mindset that looks upon all things from the perspective of What, Why, Who and How? What are you there to do? Why are you there to do it? Who is responsible, and who is accountable for doing it? And How, pray tell, do you get it done?

In each and every case above, there is a special answer to those four questions, and a general answer to those four questions.

Answer them generally, and I will show you a company struggling to get by, if even that. Answer them specially, and I will show you a company in the process of transforming their marketplace and the people who live and work in it.

Allow me to demonstrate the difference:

In the general case, the What do you do might be said, to sell and distribute light fixtures to the residential marketplace in

Detroit. In the special case, the What do you do might be said, in the very same industry, to transform the state of light fixture distribution worldwide.

In the first case, we have an ordinary business doing ordinary work in an ordinary way. In the second case, we have an extraordinary business doing extraordinary work in an extraordinary way.

The first company has a strategic objective, exactly the same objective that every one of its competitors have within that very same marketplace.

The second company has a dream, an outsized objective through which to literally transform how light fixtures are designed, built, marketed and supported, worldwide. The first company is driven by a general description. The second company is driven by a special description.

To fulfill the first company's strategic objective, general knowledge implemented efficiently and effectively will earn it a competitively secure space in its local market.

To fulfill the second company's dream, Specialized Knowledge —

Marketing Knowledge, Financial Knowledge, Enterprise Development Knowledge, Engineering Knowledge, Digital Knowledge, etc., etc., will earn it a leadership role in the worldwide community of the light fixture industry.

The difference between the two, is extreme!

The first calls for transactional skills. The second calls for transformational skills. The first is led by a transactional leader. The second is led by a transformational leader.

The way in which the people in each of those entities is inspired, led, taught, trained, managed, and developed are completely foreign to each other. Very much like a McDonald's store is remarkably different than a Starbucks store. Very much like the founder of McDonald's set out in his uniquely differentiated manner through which to design, build, launch and grow the only company of its kind in the world.

Just as did, however differently, the founder of Starbucks set out in his uniquely differentiated manner through which to design, build, launch and grow the only company of ITS kind in the world.

Astonishing, yes?

This is how we do it here, yes?

And in each of the above cases, it comes down to the very words a young women uses at the counter, to greet a new customers, to greet a returning customer, to respond to a concern any one customer might have about any one problem every single one of their customers has had, and might have, from the very first day in service, to the very day they're experiencing it, the minute by minute Special Operation of their Very Special company, doing their Very Special things they do, in their almost infinitely Special way of doing them, every single one of them, every single day, by every single employee, for one solitary, exclusively original purpose, to reinstate the McDonald's Brand, the Starbucks Brand, in the hearts and minds of those they were created to serve.

Which is after all what a Brand is, once said and done, isn't it? It's a Special Way of being in the world. And if it isn't, then what? Then failure, of course. Because that's why the vast majority of new businesses fail, 70% of all those started up in their very first year! 95% of which fail before they reach their 10th anniversary. Which then explains why Specialized Knowledge is not only important, but essential.

Because it is only Specialized Knowledge which distinguishes special companies and special people from everyone else. Welcome to the conversation. Welcome to a special new world. Welcome to a special new you!

Wishing you the most special of experiences as you visit the most special authors in this book series who follow in my footsteps in this journey.

Michael E. Gerber ~ Creator of The E-Myth.

MICHAEL E. GERBER

Michael E. Gerber is the author of the N.Y. Times mega-bestseller, for two consecutive decades, *"The E-Myth Revisited"* and nine other worldwide bestselling E-Myth books concerning small business entrepreneurship, leadership, and management.

Additionally, Michael E. Gerber has written 19 industry-specific E-Myth Vertical books co-authored by industry experts, for Attorneys; Accountants; Optometrists; Chiropractors; Landscape Contractors; Financial Advisers; Architects; Real Estate Brokers; Insurance Agents; Dentists; Nutritionists; Bookkeepers; Veterinarians; Real Estate

Investors; Real Estate Agents; Chief Financial Officers; and soon to be, HVAC Contractors and Plumbers.

His mission is "to transform the state of small business worldwide™."

CHAPTER 5

IMAGINE THE OUTCOME

"There is no life I know to compare to pure imagination. Living there, you'll be free if you truly wish to be."
~ Willy Wonka

Our minds are powerful, multifaceted biological computers. They can create or destroy with a single thought. You see this demonstrated hundreds of times on a daily basis. One of the first thoughts for many is, "I need caffeine to wake up." You go about your morning routine with the anticipated reward of your caffeine fix to keep you going for the next part of your day. The reality is you have already been functioning without the caffeine until you grasp a cup in your hand. Do you need caffeine, or do you believe you need it? Perception, reality, and IMAGINATION play integral parts in our daily lives.

In 1987, I was a young woman working as an Administrative Assistant at a credit union in Omaha, Nebraska. One of my morning tasks was to make sure there was coffee ready before everyone else arrived. I mistakenly made two batches of decaffeinated coffee. I observed as each employee dragged themselves into the office and zombie-like beelined to the break room for a cup of coffee. Their eyes were barely opened until they took their first sip. Instantly, their eyes would widen, their posture straightened, and a smile would come across their faces. One by one, I observed a mind-over-matter transformation instantly occur. These people believed caffeine was in their cups, recharging them for their day. Out of the 12 employees who drank the coffee, only one complained that they were not feeling a caffeine boost. I observed, noted, and proceeded to make another double batch of decaffeinated coffee later that day.

Why run such an experiment? First, it started as an accident. Secondly, I was an engineering student who enjoyed testing a reasonable hypothesis. After several runs of this experiment over several weeks, I discovered only one person was sensitive to the lack of caffeine. That information caused me to run other experiments around facts and IMAGINATION throughout my lifetime. What did we see versus what we expected to see, rather than what was actually there? In my college classes, I discovered if I imagined that I knew the material then walked into class, my professors would not call on me. On the other hand, if I walked in appearing clueless, I was sure to be called to the board to explain all I did not know to the class. I learned quickly to embrace the "I know this" look into the core of my existence.

Please note, perception of what is expected or has happened before has no place in pure IMAGINATION. It will cloud the possibilities. Think of your childhood. Whether you were rich or poor, happy or sad, your IMAGINATION was a source of comfort in times of need. When lonely, we created friends; bored, created adventures; stuck inside, built worlds. Regardless of your circumstances, IMAGINATION was the key to distraction and inspiration. As children, our

IMAGINATION fueled us. When asked as a child, "What do you want to be when you grow up?" how did you answer? Whatever you said, you declared with enthusiasm! I know my answer was always something to the effect of, "I'm going to be a doctor, pilot, and sing with Gene Kelly!" What did your dream job look like? Did you land anywhere close? Are you using any of the skills you admired? I'm always fascinated by people who break the perceived norms of occupations. People like:

- Brian May, guitarist for QUEEN, Song Writer, and a Ph.D. in Astrophysics.
- Hedy Lamarr, Actress, and Inventor, pioneered the technology that became WiFi, GPS, and Bluetooth.
- Arnold Schwarzenegger, Body Builder, Actor, Film Producer, businessman, Politician.
- Michael Jordan, Athlete of multiple sports and businessman.

Just because you chose one career path in your youth doesn't mean you must stay there. We grow up—our point of view shifts. Our priorities change. Dream big and outside your perceived lane. What can you use in your current job that can be applied to what you really want in life? What can you pull from your experiences that can be applied to your dream? What do your heart and mind imagine?

I remember watching the television show Star Trek back in the 1970s, thinking about how cool it would be to have a phone on my hip, talk to my room to dim the lights, and push a button to receive meals, even if it was in pill form. The kids in my neighborhood would build forts of cardboard and scrap wood that we would name different starships. We recreated worlds from neighborhood to neighborhood, and we used phrases like "Beam me up, Scottie" as someone inside the fort would drop a rope to pull us up or make us climb into our "ship." We pretended our Walkie-Talkies were flip communication devices. We wanted it all to be real. So much so that what was pure science fiction imaginary tools became a reality within our lifetime. That is the power of IMAGINATION!

I challenge you to stop seeking outside affirmations of what can and cannot be done. Close your eyes for a moment. Use your IMAGINATION to see yourself accomplish a goal. How are you receiving this accomplishment? How do you feel? What is happening around you? What are you wearing? What are you driving? What do you see? What do you hear? Smell? Taste? Now, embody those images. In your mind's eye, walk into it. You are there. Bask in the feelings. Remember what this moment feels like. Now, open your eyes and keep the overall feeling. Your task is to live every day in that feeling. Wake, eat, exercise, walk, work, talk and interact in your world holding that feeling. Live emotionally in that state. Your ideal state of existence is waiting for you to catch up to it. Keep walking. I like to say, "Live and act as if what you want has happened. You are simply catching up to it." You've probably heard or seen Dream Boards and the term "Manifestation." Each of these tools and terms helps clarify what you want in the future until it becomes a reality.

Why did I share different scenarios about perception and IMAGINATION? Because it is a large part of what I do as a professional speaker and speaker coach. You must be able to imagine the outcome. Release all preconceived notions of "what-if" and create in your mind what you want your audience to leave with. My example of walking into my college classes with an air of confidence is not "faking it until I make it." It was knowing I would understand by the time I left that class. This lesson can be used to walk into any room with confidence. See the end in mind. The examples of people who didn't limit themselves to their initial career lane prove that it can be done. Lastly, the Star Trek example proves that just because it hasn't happened before doesn't mean it can't become a reality.

IMAGINATION is the key to our future. Without playing into fantasy scenarios, there isn't progress. If you can't imagine what "it" you want, then what drives you to try? Think of this scenario: When you say some task or invention is impossible, only a few will fight to prove you wrong. On the other hand, if it is declared that a task or invention is possible, far more will strive to solve the "how" to make it a reality. Break through the mediocre. Use your IMAGINATION, dream, and make the supposedly impossible possible.

Our minds are powerful, multifaceted biological computers. They create or destroy with a thought. You might as well use that powerful thought for good. As Spider-Man's Uncle Ben wisely said, "With great power comes great responsibility."

122

EXCERPT BY ERIK SWANSON

IMAGINE THIS

"Man's only limitation, within reason, lies in his development and use of his imagination"
~ Napoleon Hill, *Think and Grow Rich*

Imagination is the beautiful creation of a mental image in our minds so powerful and astonishing that it is believed to be real. It truly is what makes the world go around in my eyes. Without Imagination, the world simply would be stagnant and at a standstill.

Napoleon Hill teaches us that there are two types of Imagination - the Synthetic and the Creative. Although both are so vitally important to our success, I would like to focus on the Creative Imagination with you today.

In fact, I have created a new concept in which I use Imagination along with three other important components; when combined, literally transforms anyone's success quotient into a fantastic proven result!

"VICI"

The concept is called "VICI," which implements four critical components: Visualization - Imagination - Creation - Implementation.

When I started working in the personal development world in my late twenties, I used to travel around the United States and Canada, training corporations and sales teams in various industries. It was a grueling job, to be honest. But it did give me the awesome opportunity to see the world, experience different cities and cultures, and meet so many individuals. It opened my eyes to so many lessons throughout those years.

One part of my job back then would be to conduct training workshops in front of strangers whom I had never met before and motivate them to take action on our company's offer for further training systems and seminars. So, if you think about it, I was a young guy in my twenties, just out of college, expected to go and train professionals who were older than me and most likely making twice the income I was at the time. To say that I was nervous at times would be an understatement.

I had to figure out a way to calm my nerves. I had to figure out a way to be the amazing and awesome individual I am and still get the fear out of the equation, at least pretend that the fear was not there. I had to do all of this without the strangers in front of me knowing what was truly going on in my mind while I stood in front of them. I was hoping they would not see the perspiration dripping from under my suit and tie.
I started to notice there was a direct correlation between my perspiration and my income. The more my fear showed to

these strangers, the more my results and my income would take a dive. You know that saying, "Sweat and Tears?" Well, I started calling it my "Sweat and Fears!"

I really needed to change this around in my favor. If I didn't figure something out and quickly, I would have to reconsider what my career choice should truly be.

The fear was even creeping into my dreams the night before. If I knew I had an appointment with a team the next morning, that night before would be a rough ride in the brain of Erik Swanson while he slept.

Then one day, it hit me! I figured it out! I decided that if I was going to dream about these strangers every night before I met them the next morning in reality, then I would start to work on my dreams and win them over there!

Why not talk to them while I'm dreaming and get to know them there so that I would not be as nervous when I meet them the next day. I started to visualize them smiling and being very welcoming to me. I began to visualize them not judging me but actually enjoying my training and embracing my techniques. I started to visualize what types of objections they would have and actually visualize myself handling those objections perfectly in my dreams. This was such a game-changer!

Then I took it to the next level and imagined them applauding my speech and training. I imagined each one of these strangers signing up for our future trainings. I imagined that I already knew each of their names. I imagined they were great friends of mine already. Imagination worked in my favor in presenting to my mind something that felt like it was already in reality.

Once I had these two components all set in my dreams the night before each and every meeting, I took it to the next level. This would be the level of consciousness. It's also what I called the Level of Creation. In the morning, when I awoke, I would walk over to the mirror while brushing my teeth and start to create the reality by repeating some amazing affirmations to myself about how this meeting will actually go.

I would say to myself things like: They love you! They respond to you in such a favorable way! They need you! They want you there with them!

I kept repeating great affirmations like this, and I would speak these words of affirmations out loud to myself. I would even thank them back out loud… even using common names. At first, it was hilarious. You could hear me saying my affirmations and then saying, "Thank you, John," "I appreciate that, Kathy," "You are so right, David!"

Once I had these three components down, it was time to suit up and conquer! Time for Implementation! I was so pumped up during my drive over to their offices that nothing could stop me — not even fear!

I would march right into their offices with a certain aura about me. People noticed that I was in such a great mood. People would start to smile at me for no reason. Everything just seemed to start flowing in such a positive way for me, no matter where I turned. Then, I started to notice that people wanted to surround themselves with this feeling and with ME!

Perfect! I'm ready! VICI was working! I started implementing all of the components while standing in front of these perfect strangers. And, wouldn't you know it, there would actually be a John, Kathy, and a David in the room somehow. Wow! Image that. I literally used the power of Imagination to create such a wonderful and beautiful environment. An environment in which I call your "PME," which stands for Positive Mental Environment. This is the environment in which we all strive to be in, yet many fail to achieve. You must subconsciously and consciously seek and create this environment.

Napoleon Hill was once asked if the art of Imagination can be learned as a skill. I am here to say it can. So, practice my VICI method and watch your results and your Imagination bring you to new successes in reality. In fact, let your Imagination go wild!

ERIK SWANSON

As an Award-Winning International Keynote Speaker and Multi-Time #1 International Bestselling Author, Erik Swanson is in great demand around the world! He speaks to an average of more than one million people per year. Mr. Swanson has the honor of having been invited to speak to many schools around the world, including the prestigious Harvard University. He is also a recurring faculty member of CEO Space International and an alumni keynote speaker at Vistage Executive Coaching. Mr. Swanson is also the recipient of the 2024 International Book Impact Award and the United States Presidential Lifetime Achievement Award presented by the White House in 2024 for his ongoing community service and philanthropy work. Erik's speeches can be found on Amazon Prime TV as well as joining the TED Talk Family with his speeches called "A Dose of Awesome" and "NDSO ~ No Drama, Serve Others."

Erik got his start in the self-development world by mentoring directly under Brian Tracy. Quickly climbing to become the top trainer around the world from a group of over 250 handpicked coaches, Erik started to surround himself with the best of the best and very quickly started to be invited to speak on stages alongside such greats as Jim Rohn, Bob Proctor, Les Brown, Sharon Lechter, Jack Canfield, Lisa Nichols, and Joe Dispenza —just to name a few. Erik has created and developed the super-popular Habitude Warrior Conferences and Speaker Hearts Mastermind & Retreats, which have a two-year waiting list and include thirty-three top-named speakers from around the world. They are "TED Talk" style events which have quickly climbed to the top ten events not to miss in the United States! He is the creator, founder, and CEO of the Habitude Warrior Mastermind, Global Speakers Mastermind, and Cafe Mastermind. He is also the creator and publisher of many book series such as *The 13 Steps To Riches* book series as well as *The Principles of David & Goliath* book series. His motto is clear: "NDSO!" No Drama – Serve Others!

CHAPTER 6

WIND BENEATH YOUR WINGS

"The universe doesn't give you what you ask for with your thoughts; it gives you what you demand with your actions. In essence, you don't get what you want; you get what you are."
~ Steve Maraboli

It is important to surround yourself with others that have strengths that you lack and whom you work harmoniously with. This group must consist of people who believe that defeat is not the end.

So far, we've acquired vastly diverse perspectives from the authors who have contributed to the prior volumes of the *13 Steps to Riches* series. Although we read the same material, the insight we gain is based on our past experiences and how we interpreted the lessons. As a result, the meaning reveals itself differently to each reader.

Regardless of which author(s) you resonate with, there comes time to initiate, plan and make your desire play out through faith, auto-suggestion, specialized knowledge, and igniting the desire into action with imagination.

What will you do now? Are you a leader or a follower? I suggest that it is time to be both. A leader of self while simultaneously being a follower of stronger leaders. We need to swing between leader and follower to reach the next level.

It's time to make a plan. Throughout the process of learning the steps in *Think and Grow Rich,* it is clear that no one is in the wealth game alone. We need to gather a group of individuals around us to achieve continually. This group of similar yet not-like-minded minds will have mastered different aspects of the process as well as those able to imagine what can be.

This mastermind of individuals must also have a can-do attitude. They are individuals that see failures as lessons to rebuild and circumvent, not cave to. We need this mindset to help each other grow past our own limiting beliefs.

Organized planning is a skill that develops out of desperate necessity. During my college days, I remember I was in a very difficult class, Differential Equations. Engineering students lovingly called it DiffyQs. That class was the bane of my existence. There were mathematical constructs that I simply couldn't grasp. I was failing the class. A few fellow students and I decided that joining our thoughts together would be the only way we could all pass the class. We met every other night at the campus library to hash through the equations for upcoming exams. DiffyQs was such a mind-blowing class that we were given four equations to solve weeks prior to an exam, and we would still fail. One equation would take twelve to fifteen pages of meticulously written formulas, one after another, to solve. Even if you solved each formula correctly, one dropped negative, a derivative not carried out to the proper decimal point would destroy every step followed. It was maddening.

It was imperative that at least four of us came together. The study sessions went deep into the night for weeks. We shared the rotation of who was the lead, much like a flock of geese. Have you ever witnessed the "V" shape of geese migrating? A lead bird breaks the wind's path for the others to form behind. At intervals, the lead bird will drop from the front and take a spot in the back of the formation. This gives the lead bird a chance to rest as another moves forward to assume the lead. Give and take, ebb and flow, lead and follow. For us, sharing the leadership role created a growth atmosphere so that each of us could share our strengths while simultaneously following the lead of another.

Where in life have you used this construct and joined forces with a group of individuals to achieve a greater goal?

Another example of organized planning in my life is when my husband and I were living overseas in Geilenkirchen, Germany. We were a young military family living in a foreign country. Many of the airmen were about our same age and were also starting families. The husbands were constantly deploying to support the NATO mission in Bosnia. That left many of the spouses together to bond and explore the continent together. All the while, we were navigating it with our young children in tow. A group of mothers would come together twice a week to compare notes on child rearing, talk to the seasoned mothers, and basically learn from each other. We shared everything from baby digestive issues, potty training, language development, and more. This form of mastermind was established so that young mothers could gain a sense of readiness for whatever life would throw their way.

**"Be stubborn about your goals
and flexible with your methods."
~ Unknown**

Never underestimate the power of a tribe. This brings me to my final example of a mastermind. As an international keynote speaker, I have traveled to exotic places and met hundreds of amazing people with stories powerful enough to change the course of other lives. The stories I have collected belong to people I felt needed a platform to share their stories. They bear witness to transformation through trauma into success.

Furthermore, these stories show that the learning curve is not linear and that sometimes we take big steps backward to take greater strides forward. The book series, *Hold My Crown - Women of Grit Share Stories of Resilience* was born out of the necessity of women helping women. This mastermind has no boundaries and no walls to confine their thoughts. Through social media, we have reached around the world with the stories of resilience. Together, we share our journeys so that others will benefit from the lessons we share regardless of where they are in their life journey or where they reside. This mastermind will not stop at one book. There are plans to create a *Hold My Crown - Kings* edition with a continued compilation of Queens and Kings joining stories for future anthologies.

A Mastermind is more than a gathering of minds. It is a construct that allows the cultivation of thoughts, ideas, and plans to move into action and results. The coming together of diverse strengths and abilities helps foster fresh ideas. Organized planning is the oxygen that feeds the flames of desire into action.

"A dream written down with a date becomes goal.
A goal broken down into steps becomes a plan.
A plan backed by action makes your dreams come true."
~ Greg S. Reid

EXCERPT BY MARIE DIAMOND

ORGANIZED PLANNING BY A TRANSFORMATIONAL LEADER

In this chapter, I wish to go deeper into how you can organize successful Transformational Leadership. I was inspired by the 10 major causes of failure in leadership and the 30 major causes of failure, both mentioned in the chapter Organized Planning in the book "*Think and Grow Rich*" by Napoleon Hill.

As a Master Teacher in the global phenomenon *The Secret*, which was partly based on the knowledge of the book *Think and Grow Rich*, I want to change the wording used in Organized Planning. Using words like failure keeps the subconscious mind focused on attracting more failure. What you focus on is what you get more of.

Transformational leadership is the leadership style of the 21st century. These leaders are inspiring positive changes in their teams and their clients. They are concerned and involved in the business process but also focus on helping their team, their clients, and the planet.

Some of the most Valuable Sources of Success with Transformational Leadership:

HAVING A PURPOSE IN LIFE

Transformational Leaders have a personal purpose, a purpose for their business, and a purpose of contributing to Humanity. When you have nothing to aim for, you will not be able to manifest a difference in your life on this planet.

ABILITY TO PUT YOUR VISION IN A DETAILED PLAN

Transformational leaders are able to take their vision and surround themself with a team to create a detailed business and marketing plan. While the leader holds the vision, (s)he is able to guide his/her team to bring together the detailed plan for the implementation and manifestation of the vision.

BEING THE BEST

Transformational Leaders are not focused on small numbers or small results because they always have a large vision and focus on the big impact of their products and services. As they know when they are the best in who they are and what they do, they will reach higher and wider than others. It is not ambition that drives them but a cause of changing the world in a positive way.

HEART OF SERVICE

Transformational Leaders bring forward products and services to make a difference to Humanity. Their heart is compassionate toward the planet and the suffering in Humanity. They will make a difference with ecological goods, planet-safe procedures, and create a diverse team around them, that supports each other. They are not asking this only from their team but use these values in every aspect of their leadership.

GENDER EQUALITY REMUNERATION

Transformational leaders pay their teams for the combination of services, solution-driven creativity, and leadership. Salaries and remuneration are not influenced by gender, race, religion, sexuality, cultural background, and other dismissive inequalities.

INCLUSIVITY IS PRIORITY

Transformational Leaders are aware of the talents and skills of their team. They ask them to use this to fulfill their own purpose and the purpose of the business that they have joined. There is no top-down business decision model, but a model of listening to the team before decisions aligned with the vision are made.

INTUITION AND IMAGINATION

Transformational Leaders are in touch with their gut feeling or their intuitive side thru spiritual practices. They are able to visualize the vision with their imagination. They are surrounded by a team that is allowed to listen to their intuition and have the ability to think outside of the box with their imagination.

GENEROSITY

Transformational Leaders are generous in honoring the work of their team with positive conversations, financial rewards, and promotions. They know that recognizing the strength of their team is more important than getting themselves all the honors and awards.

POSITIVE ATTITUDE

Transformational leaders have a positive attitude toward their vision, goals, their team, and towards the future. They encourage others to have this positive attitude too. It helps the endurance and the vitality of the circle around them.

LOYALTY

Transformational leaders are steadfast and focused on their vision and loyal to the team that supports them in building out their organization and manifesting their goals.

ENCOURAGEMENT

Transformational leaders are leading by example and encourage their team to do so too. There is no space for fear-based communication but only for encouraging others to be the best in who they are. Their conduct, sympathy, understanding, and fairness are a demonstration of their leadership skills.

OPEN COMMUNICATION

Transformational Leaders are not focused on titles, educational degrees, and backgrounds but only on the human potential of their team. They communicate openly with them with always the vision and goals as a guiding star.

THE ETERNAL STUDENT

Transformational Leaders know that they never know enough about themselves, the world, and about leadership. They will always have a mentor, a teacher, a mastermind group, and books to guide them to learn more. Self-education never stops, and it is always with respect to the others. But it is more than education; it is applying as soon as you know the information so that your learning gives you results.

MASTERING YOUR EMOTIONS AND YOUR MIND

Transformational Leaders do not lead by their ego. They have mastered their negative emotional reactions and thoughts or at least do not share them with their team. They reflect within before they have difficult conversations about team issues. Mastering Yourself is the key, or you will become the victim of your Ego.

TAKING CARE OF YOUR WELL BEING

Transformational Leaders listen to their body as it is the vessel to manifest their vision with. Good sleep, an organic and healthy diet, regular exercise, daily walks in nature, meditation, and more contribute to your good health.

KEEP MOVING FORWARD

Transformational Leaders know that there is never a time that is right; it is time right NOW. Take everyday steps forward, and the journey will bring you to Success. Do not allow procrastination to dominate your life. When the Universe has given you a vision, you have the responsibility to fulfill this vision to the best of your abilities.

PERSISTENCE, EVEN WHEN THINGS ARE GETTING TOUGH

Transformational Leaders keep their eye on the finish line: manifesting their vision. Of course, there can be difficult times, hardship, lack of money, legal issues, and so much more obstacles. But they will persist as they know there is the Light at the end of the tunnel.

WORKING AND LIVING IN A POSITIVE AND HARMONIOUS ENVIRONMENT

Transformational leaders know that you need to have a harmonious and decluttered space around you. As a Feng Shui

Master, I have been teaching this knowledge for more than 25 years. You can start this process by finding your Energy Number on my Free Marie Diamond App (Google play store and App store). Indicate your Gender and your birthday, and you will receive your Energy Number, four best compass direction, and video's how to start activating your office for Success and Abundance.

PICTURE COMPASS

Your home is the unconscious expression of yourself. When I enter a home or office, I always look for signs to see if people feel powerful. As you are the Universe within, you need to be in power in your life. When you are not in power, you are not attracting what you really desire. Instead, you will stay connected with a poor consciousness and feel vulnerable and weak. You will feel that you are the victim of your reality instead of being the master of your life.

European kings and queens to the emperors of China and all political leaders had one thing in common: they sought a long and powerful government. They wanted to be the masters of their countries.

Your life is like a country. Your wish is to be the master of yourself and to make your dreams come true. What can you change to become the master in your Universe? Here are your first steps.

STEP 1: Sit or sleep like a King or a Queen/ a President/ a Leader.

Do you see the gifts of the Universe come to you, or do you sit with your back to them? At your home or workspace, you always need to see who enters, whether from your couch, dining table desk, or anything else you work on. Make sure you sit in such a way that you can see the incoming energy.

The Universe comes through the door and not through the windows. So facing a window and having your back towards the door is not efficient. The Universe walks in when you walk in. Even if you don't have any physical people walking in, you still come in, and you are the Universe.

You are not following the Principle of Power in the Universe when you come into your home and office and see:

In your living room, you are sitting with your back to the door, watching TV or talking to your family.

In your bedroom, when you wake up, you don't see the door immediately. In your office, you are sitting at a desk, but your back is facing the entrance of your office.

In a restaurant, your back is facing the entrance of the restaurant, or your back is facing the door when eating.

Solutions:

Rearrange your couches so you can see the door. Never have someone completely sitting with their back to the incoming flow of energy.

In your Bedroom: Place your bed on a wall so you can see your romantic partner coming in. When this is not possible, place a little mirror across the incoming door so you can see who is coming the moment you wake up.

In your Office/Workspace: Place your desk so you can see people walking in. When this is not possible, place a little mirror to the right or left and in front of you so that it shows you who is coming in from behind you.

Arrive first to your dinner appointment and make sure you can see the door and your guests arriving.

STEP 2: Be Supported by the Universe All the Time.

When you consider kings, queens, and emperors, you realize they are always looking to be supported by a Higher Energy and by their people.

A king or queen will always sit on a throne that supports their back and their neck. Their arms are resting on the chair. You wish to have the same support.

A true Master of Transformation allows support from the Universe at all times because, without this support, you are unable to fulfill your dreams and manifest your true potential.

Successful people always sit on impressive high-backed chairs. They are not sitting on small chairs without back support.

You are not following the Principle of Power in the Universe when you come into your home and office, and you see:
- You are sitting on a chair with a low back.
- You are sitting on a chair with slats.
- You are sitting on an old chair that is falling apart.
- You are sitting on the ground or on a pillow
- You are sitting on a couch without support for your back.
- You are sleeping in a bed without a headboard or on a mattress on the ground.
- You are sleeping in a bed with metal or wooden slats.

Solutions:

Buy a high-backed chair and place it behind your desk, especially when your back is facing the door.

Cover the back of your chair with fabric or place a pillow between you and the back of the chair.

Remove the old chair tand purchase a new one.

Place a headboard at the end of your bed to support your head, or start by placing pillows between your head and the wall.

Place your mattress on another mattress, on bricks, or anything that brings it 30 cm or a foot from the ground.

Cover the metal and wooden slats with fabric or place pillows against the slats.

When you can't do anything like this, make sure you place support behind you symbolically: a religious, spiritual, or philosophical image or statue of support: a Saint or Angel in the Christian tradition, an image of the Letters of God, an image of a Rabbi from the Jewish tradition, the Koran from the Muslim tradition, Gurus from the Hindu tradition, Images of Gods or Goddesses, spiritual Teachers from other Eastern traditions, an image of the CEO or the president of your company, or just an image of a mountain (Not completely covered by snow).

Place a rock, a Buddha statue, an image of an angel, or any other image of support connected with your religious, spiritual, or philosophical beliefs behind your home, opposite the front door.

You can also place a large, round-leaved plant behind you for support.

STEP 3: Surround Yourself with Power

The images/statues that are hanging around you represent you. The more powerful the images/statues that are in your home or office, the more you will be treated as a powerful person.

Depending on what you wish to accomplish and in what area you wish to be powerful, your images will be different.

When you wish to be a powerful scientist, then make sure you hang an image of Einstein or Newton in your living or working space.

When you wish to be an author, place books that have been read for hundreds of years; try Shakespeare.
Make sure you resonate with the images. If you don't like the person, don't hang it up.

What are Powerful Images?

- Images of successful people in your profession.
- Images of award-winning people connected with your goal.
- Images of your idols and heroes, dead or alive.
- Images of famous people.
- Images of mountains.
- Images of your masters, CEO, or managers.
- Images of your certificates.
- Images of Buddha, Jesus, Angels, Saints, or Gurus.
- Statues of (fake) awards like an Oscar with your name on it.
- Front covers with your image on them (even if fake).
- Images of your products in a golden frame

- Images of royal or imperial figures
- Images of people you admire
- Images of your logos, ads, marketing material, articles
- Your vision board with your success goals

Where to place your Powerful Images?

Make sure you have powerful images at the entrance of your company

Place them in the North area of your office

You can hang them behind your chair to feel supported by powerful people

You can also hang them in front of where you sit to focus on these successful people

Place them in your personal success direction. Download the Free Marie Diamond App (for iPhone and smartphones available) and find out your personal energy number. You will immediately see with the Diamond Compass where your personal success direction is in the room you are standing in.

You can always place your Power affirmation in the north area of your living room, as it will impact all the people living in this home. Or you can place it in the north area of a conference room, and it will create power for the whole company.

STEP 4: Activate your personal Success Direction

You can also place more personal information about your Success and Abundance in your personal success direction. You can find your personal Success direction in the Free Marie Diamond App and with some videos to help you with implementation.

Marie Diamond, Master Teacher in The Secret and Global Renowned Feng Shui master with more than 1 million online students.

www.Mariediamond.com

Extra tips:

Make sure there is no clutter at the entrance or in the North area of your office.

Remove all images in your home that do not convey power or success.

MARIE DIAMOND

Marie Diamond is one of the world's top transformational leaders, speakers, and internationally bestselling authors. A renowned voice on Law of Attraction, Feng Shui, and Dowsing, Marie Diamond is the creator of the Diamond Feng Shui, Diamond Dowsing, and Inner Diamond Meditation Programs. A 'seer' in a modern context, Marie was the only European star featured in the worldwide phenomenon *The Secret*. Latest movies she contributes to are "*Beyond The Secret*" and "*Thoughts become Things*" in 2020.

Marie merges her profound intuitive knowledge of Energy and the Law of Attraction, with her extensive studies of Quantum

Physics, Meditation, Feng Shui, and Dowsing to transform the success, financial situations, relationships, motivations, and inspirations of individuals, organizations, and corporations. Her clients include billionaires, A-list celebrities in film and music (Steven Spielberg, The Rolling Stones, Paula Abdul, etc.), top-selling writers, motivational speakers (Rhonda Byrne, Jack Canfield, Bob Proctor, Marianne Williamson, Vishen Lakhiani, etc.), world-class athletes, leading CEOs, Fortune 500 Companies (BP-Amoco, Exxon Mobil, etc.), MLM Companies (Lyoness, WorldVentures, Nikken, Herbalife,etc.). Globally, Marie has assisted government leaders, and governmental organizations in Belgium, Kazakhstan, Russia, Iceland, USA, Canada, and Mexico by providing comprehensive advice and solutions based on her expertise.

Marie is a Founding Member of the Global Transformational Leadership Council and is both Founder and President of the Association of Transformational Leaders of Europe. Marie has established a world-class reputation for transforming the success, health, relationships, and spiritual wisdom for millions of people. She is someone that thousands of entrepreneurs, businesses, and corporations turn to for unique insights and guidance with branding, marketing, and business decisions. She is also knighted to Dame Commander for her contribution to Humanity.

CHAPTER 7
WHO'S IN CONTROL?

"Button, button, who's got the button."
~ Willie Wonka

When a plan fails, people look for someone to blame. Especially when it comes to our lives. People are quick to respond with excuses about their upbringing, lack of education, or environment. But, the reality is that the blame falls upon ourselves. We make choices. We make the final decision.

Napoleon Hill shared that successful people are not procrastinators. They own their choices, make decisions quickly and follow through. I learned this quality the difficult way. Before 2014, I was quick to make decisions but poor on the follow-through. My gut would say, "Move that way," but my self-doubt would hold me back with all the words of caution I heard from those from my past and my circle of friends. That pivotal year created an environment for me where I had no choice but to stop and evaluate all my past decisions and hope to have the ability to make future decisions.

In May 2014, I was picking my children up from school when I was involved in an automobile accident. Initially, I seemed unharmed, but after twelve days, my speech became broken.

Soon after, I lost the ability to form words. I began to randomly fall over, which led to the inability to walk without assistance. We later learned that I had obtained a traumatic brain injury. I spent what seemed to be weeks locked in my mind. The experience was both torturous and enlightening. Torturous because I wasn't able to move or speak. The world went on without me, and I was fully conscious that it had. Enlightening because I was able to reevaluate my life until that point. The realization hit hard that I had played small throughout my life. Here I was, stuck in my shell of a body, unable to move or communicate. I regretted every life decision I procrastinated upon. I cried to myself about all the opportunities that I had allowed to slip past me as I weighed the pros and cons ad nauseam. I knew that I had wasted precious time, and here I was, unable to proactively act to change my ways.

I promised God that if I were given another chance at life, I would play bigger without allowing my fear of the unknown to cripple me. Approximately two years after my accident, I gave up hope of recovery. I felt as if I was abandoned by God. I remember screaming in my head, "If you hate me so much, then kill me already. I can't live like this"! At that moment, I heard a booming voice that emanated from every cell and every molecule around me, "You're not dead yet." In that moment, I saw every failure to decide, and every moment I thought I was alone. There was someone holding me. I was never alone. I share this story often because it moves me to this day.

I felt alone, but I wasn't. I thought I would fall on my face in failure or death, but now I know that what happened to me could have been far worse. The experience was meant to shape me into more than I thought I could be. It's hard to explain, but basically, my inability to make a decision for myself, my desire to please others, and my fear of embarrassing myself caused me to be in situations I didn't want to be in. No more. I had lived my life as a spectator. I was not going to allow that to happen again.

Soon after this enlightening incident, I began physical and neurological therapies. This was not an easy journey. There were countless setbacks, two steps forward with three steps back, over and over again. The power in this recovery dance was that I had decided to do whatever possible and whatever it would take to get myself back to being self-sufficient. I didn't want to return to being who I was. Instead, I sought to be the best version of myself. Over the course of several years, my hard work paid off. I became more self-sufficient and more decisive.

During the first year of my recovery, I was invited onto the TEDx stage to share my journey. The ideas worth sharing were: 1) Have a goal but be flexible on how you reach it. 2) Eat dessert first. Life is too short to not enjoy the little things in life, and 3) "The differences between a rut and a grave are the dimensions." - Ellen Glasgow.

I declared my intentions to the world through my TEDx talk. I decided not to procrastinate and to take charge of my life, all while being flexible on how I reached my goals. I would take risks and no longer play victim to any circumstance.

Since my declaration to the world, I have altered myself mentally, physically, and spiritually. My quick decisions have launched me into the world of professional speaking, coaching others with their messaging on stage, authorship of multiple books, being an actress in several independent films, hosting talk shows, narrating books, and traveling around the world to inspire others to live their best life—Unapologetically.

Although my career took a massive upswing, the biggest transformations were in my mindset, attitude, and ability to handle stressors. What most people comment on is my physical appearance. I shed approximately 200 pounds. I explain to people who ask about my diet and exercise regime that it started with a mental shift. I had to believe I was worthy of being myself. I had been playing the role of the good daughter, sister, wife, mother, and friend. I was unhappy. I pushed all my hardships and painful memories deep inside my psyche. My brain injury forced the wall I had built in my mind to crumble. I had to face my demons. I found a counselor to talk through all the pain. It was not easy, but it had to be done. First, I had to free myself of all the thoughts of inadequacies. I had to learn to love myself regardless of my scars. Then, I had to make the decision to be the best version of myself every day. I wasn't perfect, but I did my best every day. We've all heard this statement or something similar hundreds of times within our lifetimes:

"Life is a series of choices, and all we can do is make them."
- Kamal Ravikant

Yes, we've heard it, but have you followed through completely and embodied the power of choices and making decisions? I believe I am the living embodiment of this quote. I made choices every day to wake early, meditate, exercise, drink protein shakes, see a dietician, visit with an herbalist, take my vitamins, work on my craft, get eight hours of sleep and drink more water than I thought was humanly possible. I did everything I could to feed my brain so it could heal. Throughout this journey of doing the best things for my body, I dropped 120 pounds. I felt amazing. I thought I had won the weight and mental anguish battle.

Then I was diagnosed with breast cancer. I had to start onto a more strict regimen and fight more battles with self-doubt. That was when all the surgeries began. It seems as if every six months for three years, I had another surgery as major organs fused together or began to fail. It was rough. The key to this was the biggest decision I had declared earlier. I will own the part I played in these outcomes. I will not claim to be a victim of any circumstance. I made decisions regarding my life very quickly and made adjustments to my daily life to follow through.

The power is in the DECISION. I discovered that the inability to make a decision or to procrastinate is a decision in itself. When you hesitate, give yourself time to take three deep breaths. Calm your mind. Then address the issue with the first instinct you have. That is your decision. Now, move in that direction. The worst that can happen is you're wrong, and you fall. The bonus will be that you know what doesn't work. Repeat what works, don't repeat what doesn't. You have to have a goal in life; just be flexible in how you reach it. Eat dessert first because life is too short to wait for everything to line up perfectly before you enjoy life. Lastly, stop building the dimensions of your grave. Do something different every day so you can achieve different results. Take it from my experience. Life is too short to squander. Tomorrow is not promised. Go be the best version of yourself every day and live unapologetically.

You can't control others or the circumstances, but you can control how you react. You are in control. No one else has your buttons unless you allow it.

SIGNIFICANT DECISIONS MAKE HISTORY

In *Think and Grow Rich*, the beloved Napoleon Hill states that Decision Making is the opposite of Procrastination. Most significantly, he documents through hundreds of interviews with the rich and famous that the strong, extremely successful, and wealthy people on the planet make decisions quickly and change them very slowly, while the weak, extremely average, and financially struggling make decisions slowly and change them quickly. Why?

In my experience, there are only four reasons why people choose to procrastinate and delay making decisions:

- Low sense of self-worth
- Refusal to live in the present
- Complacency
- Focus on the outcome instead of the process

BUILDING AND STRENGTHENING SELF WORTH

The implementation process required for you to become a consistent confident decision-maker begins and ends with an up-leveling of your sense of self-worth. The best example comes from the HVAC world of Heating and Air Conditioning.

In every home and office building, thermostats are installed that focus on inside conditions, measuring changes in circumstances that allow us to accurately predict and expect what the temperature will be. A thermostat is a component of an HVAC control system that senses the difference between the actual temperature and desired set-point temperature. The moment you set the thermostat, it triggers a furnace or air conditioner to run at full capacity until the desired warmer or cooler set-point temperature is reached. Then it shuts off the equipment until it's needed again.

In terms of our human set point, it is always dialed into the level of our self-esteem, sense of self-worth, and degree of personal development.

For example, how many times have we seen someone win 100 million dollars in the lottery only to be flat broke three years later? How many people do we know who go on a faddish diet and lose fifty pounds, but six months later, they have gained all the weight back and more. How often have we seen a wonderful woman do everything she knows how to do to get out of a physically and emotionally abusive relationship, only to jump back into a more devastating relationship with a bigger loser than the bum she just kicked out?

Why is this?

It is simply because of their personal thermostat. No matter what happens on the outside with money, weight, relationships, promotions of authority, ultimately, our thermostat is going to kick in to bring our outside world to match our internal set point. To accumulate more in the outside world, it is a critical unavoidable fact that we absolutely must become more on the inside. We must realize who we really are and who/what we have the potential and obligated opportunity to become.

A FAVORITE ILLUSTRATION

When Louis XVI was forced from his throne and imprisoned, his young son, the prince, was kidnapped by those who overthrew the kingdom. They thought that in as much as the king's son was heir to the throne, if they could destroy him morally, he wouldn't realize the great and grand destiny that life had bestowed upon him.

Consequently, they took him to a community far away and exposed the boy to every filthy and vile thing that life could offer. They exposed him to foods that would quickly make him a slave to appetite, used vulgar language, and constantly exposed him to alcohol, dishonesty, and all things crude, lewd, and unrefined.

For six months, he was bombarded twenty-four hours a day by everything that could drag the soul of a man into wickedness and rebellion. But never once did the young prince buckle under pressure. Finally, his captors gave up on tempting and changing him and asked why he had not submitted himself to partaking of these worldly pleasures to satisfy his most lustful desires that were his for the taking.

With a deep and confident sense of self, the boy looked his captors square in the eyes and proudly proclaimed, "I cannot do what you ask, for I was born to be a king."

We all can become great decision makers when we stop procrastinating by focusing on the process instead of the outcome, refuse to be complacent, reset our personal thermostats and remember who we were born to be!

LIVE IN THE PRESENT

The reason some people don't live in the present is because their present sucks! So, they medicate or live in the past, which causes pain, depression, regret, or a false sense of accomplishment. We all know someone who is stuck in the glory days, refusing to stop reminiscing when they threw that 40-yard touchdown pass in high school that won the game – "yep, like Uncle Rico, I was a superstar; give me more nachos and another beer! Burp!"

Why can't they see this and choose to let go and improve? It's because they continue to associate with those who force them to join them in their past. To be a consistent, positive, powerful, effective, and efficient decision maker, we must first stop procrastinating. This begins when you tell your procrastinating friends to stop dragging you into their past, reminding them that it's like robbing your old house and you don't live there anymore!

The flip side and other root cause of procrastination is to live in the future, believing that when 'this' occurs, I will be successful; when I do 'that,' I will finally be somebody. No. Living in the future creates worry, anxiety, and stress.

Napoleon Hill declared 'Thoughts Are Things' and the best anti-procrastination thoughts I know include: 'Today you have never been this old before – and today you'll never be this young again – so right now, and every right now matters. Which means no matter what your past has been, you have a spotless future. Which means you can't always control what happens, but you can always control what happens next!"

The practical application challenge to this truth is that if you sit around wondering if your glass is half empty or half full, you've missed the point. It's refillable! Thinking positively or negatively doesn't fill up the glass. The pouring does! It's easier to act your way into positive thinking than to think your way into positive action! Is this not decision-making 101?

REFUSE TO BE COMPLACENT

As a teenager, I had been a Golden Gloves boxing champion, and Muhammad Ali had been my idol. I emulated everything he did, from tassels on my boots to the Ali Shuffle and taunting jab. With fast hands and a desire to beat everybody, I was known as the "Great White Hope." Each time I fought, instead of chanting, "Danny, Danny," my friends chanted, "Dali, Dali!" Muhammad Ali truly was my hero, and I would have given anything to meet him.

Years later, in 1988, I had just finished speaking to the students of Andrews University in Berrien Springs, Michigan. I was in the Union Building signing books when I overheard some students talking about seeing Muhammad Ali on campus.

I was so excited I could hardly ask where. They informed me that he was gone, but it was no big deal because he lived there and visited the school often. When I finished the book signing, I immediately excused myself and asked the two gentlemen who were driving me around to grab a camera and take me to Ali's home. They told me I was fooling myself if I thought I could meet him.

But at that moment, I decided to at least try. Leaving no regrets is always a powerful motivator. So is a sense of urgency: I will never get this chance again! They stopped at the big white wall and giant iron gate at the edge of a long, curving driveway. The gate was open, and the sign didn't say 'No Trespassing.' Instead, it said 'Welcome,' so I decided to get out and walk the hundred yards to his beautiful home. His eighty-eight acres had previously belonged to the Chicago gangster Al Capone, and "Muhammad Ali Farms," as Ali called it, was an amazing sight.

With my heart pounding, I took a deep breath and knocked on the front door. A woman answered. I knew from photographs that she was his lovely wife. She asked, "May I help you?" I said, "Yes, ma'am. Is Muhammad in?"

She asked, "May I tell him who is calling?" Sheepishly, I replied, "Yea, Dan Clark."

She walked away, and within seconds, an imposing six-foot-three-inch, 225-pound world champion, world peace ambassador, advocate of human rights, living legend, and idol filled the entire doorway. Muhammad simply smiled his famous smile and invited me in in his quiet, breathy voice. I excused myself for a minute, sprinted to the garden to where my friends could see me, and wildly waved my arms and whistled for them to come in.

In 1988, Muhammad's Parkinson's disease had not yet taken away his speech and mobility. For the next five hours, we sat in his living room and watched his greatest fights on his big screen, with his own personal commentary, jokes, and stories. He fed us and even performed his favorite magic tricks.

At the two-hour mark, I had realized that I needed to leave to catch my flight, but I made the decision to briefly excuse myself to reschedule my flight, so I could return to this once-in-a-lifetime experience! I'm so grateful that I did.

As we were leaving, Muhammad asked if I had any questions. I replied, "Yes. You are the three-time world heavyweight champion, which means you got beat twice. Over your career, you lost a total of five times, all to inferior opponents. Why?"

Muhammad's answer taught me the number one cause and only solution to eliminating complacency in our lives, "When you start looking at yourself as the competition and attempt to live off your past laurels and successes, you lose your competitive advantage and eventually lose the fight. Once the fight begins, you no longer hold the title but have put it up for grabs. You must do everything in your physical, mental, emotional, and spiritual power to win it back. Every time you climb in the ring, you must be brilliant at the basics, having outworked and out-prepared your opponent as a hungry, fiercely focused warrior willing and able to fight as hard as you did the first time you won the title - throwing every punch with power and purpose to do whatever it takes to win the title back!"

A paraphrased Theodore Roosevelt quote reminds us, "It is not the undecided critic or complacent who count. The credit belongs to the one who has made the decision to continually enter the arena, whose face is marred by dust and sweat and blood; who strives valiantly, errs, and comes short again and again, because there is no effort without error and shortcoming; who at best knows the triumph of high achievement, and who at the worst, if he fails, at least fails while daring greatly, so that his place shall never be with those cold and timid souls who neither know victory nor defeat."

PROCESS VERSUS OUTCOME

Stay In Process – exchanging your focus on future outcomes for an extreme focus on the present action steps that will make the projected event and desired result probable.

Stop acting as if life is a rehearsal. Live this day as if it is your last. Whatever the present moment contains, accept it like you chose it, and work with it, not against it. Realize deeply that the present moment is really all you have. Excellence and greatness are achieved when you make Now the primary focus of your life!

Instead of fixating on the future outcomes – stay in the process and do those things at the moment that are necessary to achieve the projected outcome. Then, when you do, your desired results will come!

We saw this Decision-Making ability illuminated and in action on the same weekend during the National Football League Divisional Playoff Games, in which four playoff games came down to the very last play. Think about that. From an actuarial sense, the odds against that are immense to have every game come down to the final play.

Do you remember the game between the Buffalo Bills and the Kansas City Chiefs? A combined 25 points were scored in the game's last two minutes! Bills quarterback Josh Allen battled it out with Patrick Mahomes.

With 1:54 left to play in the game: The Bills take their first lead since the first quarter. DECIDING to go for it on a fourth down and 13 to go - Allen throws a touchdown pass.

Score: Bills 29 - Chiefs 26.

Buffalo's Center Mitch Morse said: "I wish you could have been in that fourth down huddle. It was just a lot of love. Guys saying they loved each other, 'Let's execute, let's do this for each other.'"

1:02 to go: Chiefs quarterback Mahomes DECIDES they need to march 75 yards down the field to score. In five plays that took only 52 seconds, Patrick finishes by DECIDING to throw a 64-yard touchdown pass to retake the lead. Score: Chiefs 33 - Bills 29.

0:13 to go: Allen DECIDES to drive his Bills 75 yards in 6 plays, throwing a touchdown pass to get within seconds of advancing to the AFC title game. Score: Bills 36 - Chiefs 33

With 13 seconds left on the clock, Mahomes DECIDES to drive his Chiefs 44 yards on 19 yards and a 25-yard pass. Kicker Harrison Butker (who had missed the previous kick) DECIDES to tie the score with a 49-yard field goal. Score: Bills 36 - Chiefs 36—the game goes into overtime.

Bills quarterback Allen never gets another chance as Mahomes & Co. DECIDE to drive 75 yards in 8 plays, with Patrick throwing an 8-yard touchdown pass to win the game and Divisional Championship! Final score: Chiefs 42 - Bills 36

After the game, Chiefs All-Pro receiver Tyreek Hill said: "Nobody panicked. Nobody was like, 'Oh, the game is over with 13 seconds left.' We just went out and DECIDED to make plays, and the rest is history. We have a great head coach, a great offensive coordinator, and obviously a great quarterback and playmakers. All of us made critical DECISIONS that allowed us to win!"

What's important in life is resilience. It's the ability to bounce back. It's the ability to have reverses. And then an inherent sense of optimism. Can you see the light at the end of the tunnel? If there's a barn filled with defecation and pony poop, can you imagine there's a pony in there somewhere?

The ability to be resilient and take the inevitable reverses that life throws at all of us is key. It's simple and nothing more than Decision Making 102 - preparing yourself so you can positively respond to rapid change!

At the end of the day, in every industry, every profession, and every personal and professional circumstance, you don't rise to the occasion under pressure. You fall to the level of your training. This means the pressure is not something that is naturally there. It's created when you question your own ability. When you know what you've been trained to do, there is never any pressure. That's why you continuously train, prepare and practice so hard!

REMEDY

Seek counsel, not opinions. When it comes to making important decisions, let us never forget: some things are true whether you believe them or not; everybody is entitled to an opinion, but nobody is entitled to the wrong facts; you shouldn't believe everything that you think! Who do we trust in our world of fake news, with multiple contradicting opinions causing confusion and uncertainty? Is trust not at the heart and soul of decision making? Is trusting ourselves not at the heart and soul of making a decision?

Trusting ourselves begins when we acknowledge that every person born into this world was born with an inherent ability to discern good from evil and recognize right from wrong. We commonly call this ability our conscience, which means our conscience will never fail us. Only our desire to follow it decreases as we continue to do the wrong thing.

To illustrate, you and I were joined by a group of people. We entered a room that smelled so bad that our eyes teared up, and we collapsed into automatic gag reflex. But after only ten minutes in the room, it suddenly no longer smelled. Why? We had become desensitized, and the rank, smelly room was now the new normal. Is this not happening in our world of fake news where everybody with a phone has an opinion?

It's obvious that we become the average of the five people we associate with the most. So if you hang around five negative, whining, blaming, and complaining people, you will become the sixth. If you hang around with five obese, broke people who refuse to make responsible decisions about health, exercise, nutrition, and staying out of debt, you will become the sixth who can't decide to choose juice over soda and savings over credit card jail!

To become a great, confident, and consistent decision maker – especially courageous enough to make tough decisions that go against the status quo flow – the process is simple: not easy, but clear and doable when we get the facts, the whole, complete truth, both the pros and cons. Study and learn everything we can about the subject or case in point. Counsel with unbiased experts. Ponder. And most importantly, stay true to your conscience by staying in tune with your natural intuition. It's called trusting your 'gut,' realizing that most of our significant and monumental decisions are usually our first choice, made quickly and intelligently by listening to our 'still small voice' of conscience, illuminated through intuitive promptings, made possible because of our strong 'thermostat' sense of self-worth, commitment to being present in every moment, refusal to be complacent, and focus on the process instead of the outcome.

DAN CLARK

Dan Clark is the founder and CEO of an International Leadership Development Company; a High-Performance Business Coach; New York Times Best Selling Author of 35 books; a University Professor; a Primary Contributing Author to the *Chicken Soup for the Soul* series; International Podcaster; Gold Record Songwriter; and an Award-Winning Athlete who fought his way back from a paralyzing injury that cut short his football career.

Dan was inducted into the National Speakers Hall of Fame — and has been named one of the Top Ten Motivational Speakers In The World.

Dan has spoken to over 6 million people, in all 50 states, in 71 countries, on 6 continents, to more than 6,000 audiences, including most of the Fortune 500 companies, Super Bowl Champions, NASA, and our Combat Troops in Iraq, Afghanistan, Asia, and Africa.

Dan has appeared on over 500 television and radio shows, including *Oprah* and *Glenn Beck*, *PBS*, and *NPR*, and has been featured in the *Mayo Clinic Journal*, *Forbes, Inc.*, *Success*, *Entrepreneur*, *Thought Masters,* and *Millionaire Magazines*.

Dan's extraordinary life includes soaring to the edge of space in a U2 Spy plane; flying fighter jets with the Air Force Thunderbirds; racing automobiles at Nürburgring and sailboats in Australia; serving on the Olympic Committee, and carrying the Olympic Torch in the Winter Games, and keynoting the United Nations World Congress.

Dan was named an Outstanding Young Man of America - and has since received the United States Presidential Medal presented by President Ronald Reagan; the United States Distinguished Service Medal presented by the U.S. Department of Defense; he was the national recipient of the prestigious Air Force American Spirit Award, and was named Utah Father of the Year!

CHAPTER 8
GET THE COOKIE

"Believe in yourself and all that you are. Know that there is something inside of you that is greater than any obstacle."
~ Christian D. Larson

"One of the most common causes of failure is the habit of quitting when one is overtaken by temporary defeat."
~ Napoleon Hill

Perseverance is the basis of all success. You can have the greatest and most profound ideas and talent, but if you fall, which most assuredly you will, and you refuse to get back up, your ideas and talent are wasted.

It is imperative that you move toward your goal despite whatever disruptions are set in front of you. You must persevere and find your way. Be like water in a stream when an object blocks its flow: go over, around, under, or through. Perseverance will find or create a path.

May 2014 began my journey to recognize the power of perseverance. I was involved in an auto accident that left me with a multiple-area traumatic brain injury resulting in my inability to speak or walk without assistance for over two years. This experience brought me to my breaking point. The physical trauma from the accident paled in comparison to the immense emotional and mental trauma of facing my inner critics. I was locked in my mind and forced to answer all the questions and accusations of playing small and chasing the safe paths in my life thus far. This mental battle was fought alone; the old me against the new me who wanted to emerge. Two incredibly stubborn forces were battling for dominance within my mind. Through these battles, I realized that although I persevered through many obstacles, I had completely avoided the challenges that would have forced me to step into my God-given gifts and truly shine as the leader I was meant to be.

Being a captive in my body and mind was my personal version of Hell. I had to take brave steps toward healing the parts of my mind and body that were out of alignment. I had to consciously take actions to heal my mind, and in turn, my body would follow. I asked to be brought to a neurologist, where my cognitive healing began. I persevered through my neurological tests and multiple therapies despite the extreme exhaustion that would knock me out for a week at a time. I got back up. My family ensured that I would be brought to the next test or therapy over and over again. Eventually, I was released to drive myself. Years went by, and I kept pushing to the next set of neurological milestones. I sought alternative therapies to help the healing process and build new neuropathways for my injured brain.

Perseverance paid off. I weaned myself from the pain, migraine, vertigo, and nausea medications. I replaced all the pills with meditation, vitamins, a healthy diet, water, and more sleep. I became relatively independent again. I say relatively because I had to understand the new limits for my brain capacity. If I pushed my cognitive skills too much, my mind would shut down for a few days. In extreme cases, it would shut down my motor functions. I persevered through learning my limits and then pushing those limits further every time.

I remember when I did my TEDx talk in late 2015. At the time, I still had a sixteen-second short-term memory. I had recorded my talk and listened to it repeatedly in order to remain partially on course during my time on stage. In essence, I moved my talk from short-term to long-term memory. The challenge came in my ability to remain cognizant past one PM. The average human brain takes in millions of data throughout the day. My injured brain was unable to sort and ignore non-essential data absorbed. So by one PM, my mind wanted to shut off. I was scheduled to be the closing speaker at my TEDx event. I miraculously made it to my scheduled speaking time and was told I did a fantastic job, but I didn't remember what I said. Unfortunately, that experience knocked me out of commission for several weeks. Once I regained my balance, I had to persevere. At the same time, I continued to recover and relearn the sensitive art of being upright.

In late 2017, as I was almost accustomed to my two steps forward and one step back recovery process, I was diagnosed with breast cancer. My short-term memory was a blessing and a curse. I kept forgetting I had cancer. I thought I was still awaiting test results, so the full impact never really caught up to me until sixty days after diagnosis, when the surgeons performed a bilateral mastectomy and removed all traces of cancer. At that time, I was hyper-aware that I had cancer but blissfully unaware of how dangerously close I could be to death. It was as if that part of my brain was also damaged.

Nevertheless, I am thankful that I was handed a huge setback in this journey called life. I didn't let it stop me. I became very purposeful about what I needed to do next to leave my mark on the world. I had my TEDx as an accolade. The day after my bilateral mastectomy, I was telling a story at a local story-telling event broadcast live on National Public Radio. Soon afterward, I was on a plane to the John Maxwell Team conference to receive a JMT Culture Award for Attitude. I was nominated and won against over 8000 Maxwell coaches worldwide. Next, I was off to New Delhi, India, to accept my Inspirational Woman of Excellence Award from the Women Economic Forum. These travels weren't all comfortable. I had to persevere through a lot of post-surgical body pains and succumb to my body's need to rest, recovery, and be quiet, all while traveling, being amongst the crowds of conference attendees, and speaking to the masses to share inspiration. I returned home delighted with all that had transpired in my life but had a new series of physical complications initiated by the cancer.

I was back in surgery every six months to remove, adjust or disconnect a different organ. Most individuals would have been exhausted by the constant surgeries. Once again, my inability to remember and my loss of the concept of the passing of time was a blessing and a curse. I would forget that I had surgery, cause myself a lot of discomforts and completely forget the pain of the previous surgeries. There wasn't fear attached to the experiences because I didn't remember. The memory loss helped fuel my perseverance. I would wake each day looking for my next task to tackle and be ready for each day as if it were my last day on Earth.

I woke up happy, energetic, and excited to conquer something new.

I believe it was during my first surgeries when I first truly tapped into my toddler mindset. I simply refused to stay down. Nothing depressed me. I saw everything as a fun goal to complete. Think of the mindset of a toddler. Have you met a toddler that believed in defeat? Probably not. Imagine you are in a room with a toddler, and you have cookies you do not want that toddler to eat. The toddler sees the cookies and asks for one. You say, "No, these cookies are not for you." Then you place the cookies at the highest place in that room, well out of reach of the toddler. The toddler will watch you place the cookies and appear to be defeated. They may even pout or cry a bit. Now, leave the room. Wait a good ten minutes and return. I can almost guarantee that the toddler will have at least one cookie in their mouth. Then you will see the convoluted piling and series of climbing tools the toddler left in their wake as they found a way to reach the cookies. That is the toddler mindset in action: Their goal (in this case, a cookie) may be blocked or out of reach. It may initially frustrate them, but they will find a way over, around, under, or through despite the enormity of the obstacle.

Now, think of yourself. When it comes to your goals, are you as stubborn as a toddler to reach them? How often do you allow obstacles to hinder your progress? God has enabled each of us early in life to learn that we must be persistent to achieve our goals. It is our job to embrace our toddler mindset and recall that we have what it takes to get whatever cookie our life circumstances seem to withhold from us. Be as stubborn and persistent as a toddler. That childlike mentality is what we need to see outside of the box we've succumbed to. The toddler within you holds the answers to dreaming big, living fully, and reaching our goals. GET THE COOKIE.

EXCERPT BY ALEC STERN

NO MEANS NOT NOW

Throughout my life, I have been persistent in my wants and desires. I found that if I balanced this with an action plan and didn't give up, I could reach almost any goal. I have worked hard and never had anything handed to me. At times challenges can weigh anyone down to the point of wanting to give up, but I learned how to overcome these feelings and keep my mindset and drive to win.

At 2 ½ years old, I was diagnosed with Perthes Disease, an issue with hip joint development and a lack of blood flow from the hips to the legs. This required a "no activity" lifestyle to let my hip bones grow and catch up. On average, it can take between 2-6 years to make this adjustment. When I was diagnosed, the treatment was simple: no walking, no running, and no physical activity, as this could aggravate my joint development and healing process. From 2 ½ to 5 ½ years old, I was confined to braces, crutches, and a wheelchair. My family traveled back and forth from Connecticut to Boston, where I spent about half of my young life at Children's Hospital for supervision and care.

Imagine not being allowed to walk or stand up at that age! While the diagnosis was very concerning, the aggressive "no activity" treatment had a very good probability of allowing my body to heal itself, and I could go on to live a normal life. As you can imagine, going through this was very difficult for my family and me. It really required me to develop the right mindset, desire, and determination at a very young age. There were times I felt defeated because I couldn't play like other kids, but with my desire to heal, I remained persistent. The doctors and my parents assured me that if I followed the regimen, I could overcome this. So I visualized myself running and playing like all the other kids. And, at 5 ½ years old, I outgrew my hip issue to go on and live a normal life.

On the lighter side, as I grew a bit older, on any given hot summer day, I would ask my mom for an ice cream. Her usual response was no. It would ruin my appetite; I would get a cramp swimming, I had ice cream yesterday, etc. My motto then, and to this day, is "no means, not now." As I visualized enjoying an ice cream cone, I went to work on the steps I needed to achieve this outcome. I would help my mom with a project she was working on or check off a few of my assigned chores. Then I would ask again, "mom can I have an ice cream?" Her response was, "dear, you have been so helpful today; yes, you can have an ice cream."

Today, in life and business, I use this mantra of "a no means not now." Often, when you receive a no, it can be the way in which you present what you are asking for. Perhaps it is an inopportune time for a myriad of reasons. Obviously, when you get a "no," it can be frustrating and feel like a failure.

Sometimes we can be fearful of why we received a no, or we may want to blame others, thinking that they just didn't get it.

Instead, consider feedback a gift. If you ask for feedback as to why the person said no, they may share important insights with you. Or, they may prefer to not share any feedback with you. If you don't get the outcome you want from a conversation, ask if they would be open to sharing updates with you going forward. You can ask them their preferred frequency and method of communication for the updates you will provide. This allows you to cultivate the relationship and leave the door open. Over time, you can convert these no's into yes's. In many situations with potential customers, partners, investors, mentors, etc., with time and follow-up, I converted their initial "no" into a "yes," and we ended up partnering in business. This approach can also be used in life beyond business as well. In meeting and talking with others, if you set your intentions for a specific outcome and you visualize this outcome happening, you are setting yourself up for success.

Here's another example: as I finished college and started to seek out companies to potentially work for, I had an experience that took a definiteness of purpose, desire, and persistence to bring to fruition. Looking back, I am not sure I would have the chutzpah to do this today.

While in my senior year at the School of Management at Syracuse University, I was living in New Jersey. My mom was originally from Boston, and, as a young boy, we spent summer vacations and holiday breaks visiting relatives. I would often say I was going to move to Boston one day, and I visualized my doing so after graduating college.

In one of my college marketing classes, we did a case study on a hot computer company called Prime Computer that was based in Boston, Massachusetts. Prime was a new company and the first in a new space called minicomputers. Even though the company was new, they were well-funded and had filed for their Initial Public Offering (IPO). Mentioning Prime to my dad, his response was, "Who is that? You need to work for a large, established company like IBM!"

After learning about Prime Computer, I decided I wanted to work for them, so I set out to see how I could get hired by Prime. My first move was to cold call the corporate office in Boston. I asked to speak to the executive of Worldwide, Sales & Marketing. (Who in their right mind as a senior in college would cold call a senior executive at a major corporation to ask for a job? Me!) I called and was connected to his executive assistant. After stating my reason for the call was to talk about being hired for a job, I was told by his executive assistant that they were only hiring people with a minimum of 5 to 10 years of experience. She asked me where I lived. When I said New Jersey, she shared how Prime had a regional office in New Jersey, and I should contact them in a few years. I did not accept this response as I believed they would miss a big opportunity to hire recent college graduates. After many attempts and becoming friendly with his assistant, I finally got a 30-minute meet and greet. I visualized my meeting with the

Worldwide Sales & Marketing Executive for Prime and us shaking hands when he offered me a job.

The early morning of the day of my interview, I drove to Boston from New Jersey in a heavy rainstorm. I arrived 15 minutes before my appointment. I headed inside to check-in. Unbeknownst to me, my raincoat was shut outside of my car, dragging alongside my car door for the entire ride. Getting out of the car, I was met with the bottom of my raincoat covered in mud which splattered across my pant leg. I went inside and asked the receptionist (who laughed at my mess) to use the restroom. Stepping into action, I proceeded to wash my pants in the sink and attempted to dry my pants with the bathroom hand dryer. I ended up going to my interview in soaking-wet pants.

Luckily, everyone seemed to find this funny, so, despite my mishap, they were impressed and asked me to come back for another round of interviews. On my second drive up to Boston, I arrived 45 minutes early. I felt very confident, so I decided to look at apartments in the area. I stopped at an apartment complex and parked in the visitor parking lot to run in and grab some information. I left the car running as I thought I would only be a few minutes. When I came outside, I was surprised to find that I had locked myself out of the car while the car was running with my wallet sitting on the front seat of the car. I ran back inside and called a towing service. I begged them to come immediately. I now had only 25 minutes until my interview. The tow truck arrived and said that they couldn't open the car without a police officer present because I didn't have any identification. We waited for the police to arrive, leaving me only 10 minutes until my interview. The police officer said he couldn't allow the opening of the car without my providing my ID, which was locked in the car. After being very persistent, the policeman allowed the door to be opened, and I could show my ID. I then raced to the interview and pulled into the parking lot with 2 minutes to spare before my interview. My interview went well, and they asked me to come back. As an aside, my car was low on gas, and my leaving it running while waiting to get the door opened, I arrived at the Prime parking lot with only fumes of gas in the tank. After my interview, I had to walk to a gas station and purchase a filled gas can so I could drive the car to fill up for my return trip to New Jersey.

During the entire interview process, I had four visits to Prime over 2 months. Each visit for my interviews had challenges that I overcame one by one. On my last visit, we shook hands, and I was hired as the first-ever recent college graduate hired by Prime Computer! My desire and persistence had carried me through this process. No challenges or obstacles could get in my way or slow me down.

Initially, I was placed in the Prime training department to complete all the current trainings to see what resonated with me as a recent college graduate. I was tasked to help determine what was needed to build a curriculum for other recent college graduates to follow.

After 3 months in the training department, I was asked what city I wanted to be placed in for a sales/business development position, and my choice was Boston. I was assigned to a manager and team in the Boston office and was scheduled to start in two weeks. Arriving early, extremely excited and eager to start, my new boss called me into his office and asked me to close the door. With an angry tone, he said I was a liability to him and the team and that I had taken a requisition away from him that would have allowed him to hire a seasoned person with 5-10 years of experience. He went on to tell me "not to bother him or the other salespeople with questions." I was on my own. He said he would assign me some past customer accounts and territory and said, "Good luck."

At first, I felt deflated as it seemed I was set up for failure. I quickly changed my perspective and mindset and, instead, focused on how lucky I was. I set out to prove to all the executives who agreed to hire me that they made the right decision. Calling into the old customer accounts, there was resistance and, in a few cases, some laughter with comments like "why would we work with your company again?" So I started a dialogue with several company executive assistants and began to create a rapport with them. I then visualized meeting with these executives and shaking hands to do business together.

In one potential customer situation, I had been asking the executive assistant to set up a meeting with the decision-maker for a few months. When I would call, she would recognize my number and would respond with, "Hello, Alec. He still will not meet with you." I decided this time to press her for the reason he would not meet me. With persistence, I said, "I want to book a meeting, and all I ask is for 30 minutes of his time." She said, "You can't meet with him!" I said, "Why not?" She said, "Because he is out of the country for 2 weeks." I said, "Fine… I'll hold!" She asked to put me on hold. She then came back on the line and asked me, "Are you really going to hold on the line for 2 weeks?" I said, "Yes, I will hold." She put me back on hold again and then came back and said, "That was the funniest response I have ever heard. I will book a 30-minute meeting upon his return." She later shared she had a good laugh with the other executive assistants. After taking some ribbing from the executives, building a great rapport, and not letting up on my desire to do business with them, I ended up signing them as a customer and doing business together for several years.

At the completion of my first year in sales and business development, I was the overall company's "Rookie of the Year," outperforming all first-year new hires, including the new hires with 5-10 years of experience. I was also one of the "Top Sales Performers" overall, reaching more than 130% of my annual goal.

Given my success as the first, Prime went on to hire 80-100 recent college graduates annually, and I delivered the keynote speech at all the follow-on new hire training programs.

Through these challenges and many others, I've learned how to manifest outcomes by setting my intentions, creating a plan for the desired outcome, and visualizing the results I want. I don't let anything get in my way, either subconsciously through self-doubt or by external forces. For me personally, I lead with humor to keep things light and fun. By using this approach to pave a path to achieve your goals and desires, they can come true.

ALEC STERN

"America's Startup Success Expert"

Alec Stern is an entrepreneur, speaker, mentor, and investor. He has become known as "America's Startup Success Expert" for performing hundreds of keynote speeches worldwide and for his popular sessions at top conferences.

He's been a co-founder or founding team member of 8 startups with 5 exits—2 IPOs and 3 acquisitions. As a primary member of Constant Contact's founding team, Alec was one of the original 3 who started the company in an attic. Alec was with the company for 18 years, from startup to IPO, to a $1.1 Billion-dollar acquisition.

Recently, Alec was selected to the Influence 100 Authority List by Influence Magazine and was recognized as The World Authority for Entrepreneurship by The Credible Source. In 2020, Alec was a 2-time Visionary Award and a Legend Award winner for his success as an entrepreneur and for his work helping startups and entrepreneurs. In 2021, Alec was a 2-time Award of Excellence – Keynote Speaker recipient at top conferences.

One of the Northeast's most accomplished entrepreneurs, he is a limited partner in Boston-based G20 Ventures, which provides early traction capital for East Coast enterprise tech startups. Alec is also an angel investor and mentor in a number of rising startups in various industries. Today Alec is innovating in a variety of industries like SaaS, Technology, Web 3.0, Metaverse, Crypto, Medical Devices, and Cannabis.

Alec is passionate about small business, entrepreneurship, and innovation. Working within the inner cities, or as he calls it, "urban innovation," is near and dear to his heart.

Only a sideman when it comes to music, Alec is an accomplished drummer and has had the honor of sitting in with a number of musicians, including Toby Keith's house band in Vegas.

CHAPTER 9

THE MULTIPLIER OF ABUNDANCE

"Belonging is one of the most basic needs that every person has…If you desire to be a better leader, develop an other-person mindset. Begin looking for ways to include others."
~ **John C. Maxwell,** *Becoming A Person of Influence*

Do you consider yourself a lone wolf? Many small business owners and entrepreneurs tend to begin with that thought in mind. I know I did. I set out alone when I began my professional speaking and leadership coaching business years ago. My pack was the Toastmasters International family and political campaign circles. They both work in groups to achieve goals and win elections. So, when I declared I was going to take this speaking show on the road, I was told, "good luck" and patted on the back…a lone wolf without a pack to fall back upon. It was terrifying to set my sights on various speaking engagements knowing that I had to rely on my brain power, intuition, business skills, past experiences, and ability to adapt. No one I knew had walked this path of professional speaking.

I quickly realized that I needed something beyond my stellar speaking skills. I needed a product beyond myself. Did I figure that out by myself? Not at all! I learned it from a friend who invited me to join the John Maxwell Team (JMT) of certified coaches. I joined a pack closer in alignment with my professional speaking lane. He was my first co-wolf. Once I attended the JMT certification, my pack grew immensely! These were people, new family, that also had aspirations to grow as professional speakers. We would talk late into the night about our shared experiences in professional speaking and, soon, the coaching world. The ability to share knowledge with those who had "been there, done that" and provide insight from my cultural and specific educational background was a catalyst for the immense growth of my business. This interaction served me for several years, and I built strong bonds with a few of the coaches. We still meet to bounce ideas and share acquired knowledge in our perspective fields.

One day, one of my close JMT coaching friends said, "I wish we could bring our Mastermind back together." I responded, "What Mastermind?" He responded with laughter, "What do you think we were doing on our calls? We were a Mastermind group." My mind had never considered what we did together a Mastermind. We just shared what we learned through experience, education, or intuition. I had coined the meetings as our Wolf Pack time. In *Think and Grow Rich*, Napoleon Hill described the Mastermind principle as "The coordination of knowledge and effort between two or more people who work towards a definite purpose in a spirit of harmony...no two minds ever come together without thereby creating a third, invisible, intangible force, which may be likened to a third mind". My fellow coach and friend enlightened me about the concept of a Mastermind.

That was my introduction to Masterminds. I had been in one that set my business afloat, and I had no idea. I became a part of yet another Mastermind with a group of coaches that attended a retreat with Dr. Paul Scheele of Scheele Learning Systems. Wowzah! What an amazing experience. People from all walks of life, countries, and age groups came together with the goal of accelerating better outcomes for our professional and personal lives. Together, we helped envision and create paths for our success. This was a new level of Mastermind. In this group, I realized that diversity of background was essential to massive growth. Through the years, the group is still together. A few have come and gone, but the core still remains.

More recently, I became associated with a man I met by coincidence at the Ultimate Speaker Competition in Orlando, Florida. While I was in the middle of the competition, he approached me and complimented my speaking and storytelling skills. I thanked him and continued with the speaking competition. Later, he approached me again to invite me to be in a book called *the DOSE of HOPE* for his 501c3 KEEP SMILING Movement. I agreed, wrote my chapter, and submitted it. He then requested time to speak with me via Zoom. When we got on the video call, something shifted. He shared what his book was about and why he wanted me to submit a story. I shared more about my background and the short story I submitted for the book.

There was a different level of synergy that occurred. We were in alignment with what we wished to bring to the world. I believe everyone has a story that must be shared regardless of how "not tragic" or "tragic." There is someone waiting to hear that someone else experienced what they experienced or that the world is not as horrible as social media shows us. The people of the world need HOPE (Hold On Pain Ends). We both believe that this can be done one story at a time. I share my stories, written and spoken. He helps people build a legacy by publishing those stories in collaboration books for more exposure. Double WOWZAH!

Since this meeting, we have become co-creators of Ampifluence - Amplify Your Influence - "You're the Expert, but are you struggling to monetize your Authority?" This has become the ultimate Mastermind, in my opinion. We travel across the United States and, soon, abroad to meet with authors, speakers, coaches, and influencers from all areas of business to share their authority with the people in their own areas, highlight them in a book based on their geographic area and share thoughts, missions and growth plans to expand their circle into other geographic areas. We Amplify who they are and tie them to other influencers, so we all grow our influence together. The beauty of this system and process is that we have created Masterminds in each geographic area, then tie them to the next geographic area. In essence, we are building satellite Mastermind groups that tie to one larger Amplifluence Mastermind!

I discovered through this process with my co-founder, Ken Rochon, known as "Dr. Smiley," that a Mastermind does not require a large group to be effective. The two of us were a

Mastermind that developed and grew our individual businesses exponentially and drew on our satellite Mastermind groups to collaborate when we saw a possibility of collaboration. As a result, there has been massive growth amongst those who have joined us in this endeavor. We are constantly expanding and acquiring more people into our Amplifluence Mastermind family.

My question to you is, "Who are you masterminding with?" It can be anyone who doesn't think like you. Who is a good candidate: your spouse, friend, associate, networking partner, or like, in my case, a person you randomly meet at a speaking competition. The key is to bring minds together with different skill sets, perspectives, and positive mindsets. Thoughts you have had and have brushed off as unworkable can be heard by another, refined, and become exactly what you were seeking. You just need another set of brain cells to examine it. Together, you can polish the idea to make it a gem. Start with two people, then expand. Build your third master brain.

"1 + 1 = 11!"
~ Sharon Lechter, *Think and Grow Rich for Women*

THE POWER OF MASTERMINDS

Greetings! You have the opportunity now to dramatically increase your ability to earn and keep more money than you ever thought possible.

The richest and most influential people in America and probably the world have all discovered the incredible power of the "Mastermind." In interviewing wealthy people, they all recall that the turning point in their road to great success and achievement was when they formed one or more Masterminds.

Each rich person recalls the "turning point" in their life and fortunes. It was the same for all of them. It was when they started to cooperate and work with other successful people.

Many people struggled for years until that magical turning point when they met and began to share ideas with other successful people. Suddenly they were able to tap into the knowledge, experience, and skills of others. In almost no time, their ability to move ahead doubled or tripled – almost overnight.

The key to forming Masterminds is to look around yourself for one or more successful people and then determine how you can help them.

The key to tapping into the "Mastermind Principle" is to look for ways to "Give" before you get. The law of "sowing and reaping" says, "whatsoever ye sow, that also shall ye reap." This is a universal principle that works 100% of the time.

You have complete control over your future and your success without limit. But remember, the only part of this universal law you can control is the "putting in." The riches and rewards will come to you automatically, by "Law," not by chance.

From this day forward, look for ways to put in, to give of yourself. The riches and rewards will come to you faster and greater than you ever thought possible. Go for it!

BRIAN TRACY

Brian Tracy is Chairman and CEO of Brian Tracy International, a company specializing in the training and development of individuals and organizations. Brian's goal is to help you achieve your personal and business goals faster and easier than you ever imagined.

Brian Tracy has consulted for more than 1,000 companies and addressed more than 5,000,000 people in 5,000 talks and seminars throughout the US, Canada and 70 other countries worldwide. As a Keynote speaker and seminar leader, he addresses more than 250,000 people each year.

He has studied, researched, written and spoken for 30 years in the fields of economics, history, business, philosophy and psychology. He is the top selling author of over 70 books that have been translated into dozens of languages.

He has written and produced more than 300 audio and video learning programs, including the worldwide, bestselling Psychology of Achievement, which has been translated into more than 28 languages.

He speaks to corporate and public audiences on the subjects of Personal and Professional Development, including the executives and staff of many of America's largest corporations. His exciting talks and seminars on Leadership, Selling, Self-Esteem, Goals, Strategy, Creativity and Success Psychology bring about immediate changes and long-term results. Brian Tracy is the recipient of many awards including The Habitude Warrior Lifetime Achievement Award.

He has traveled and worked in over 107 countries on six continents, and speaks four languages. Brian is happily married and has four children. He is active in community and national affairs, and is the President of three companies headquartered in Solana Beach, California.

CHAPTER 10
I AM WOMAN

When I was a little girl in the Philippines, my grandfather sat me on the ground and explained to me that we are all energy. He guided me to pray to connect with the spirit and God. He had me focus on the warmth from the ground and feel it travel through my body into my heart. That was when I was to pray and connect directly to the source. This exercise in energy and spiritualism was my introduction to transmutation.

Later, as a teenager, I read, *Think and Grow Rich*. When I reached the chapter regarding Transmutation, the song, *I Am Woman*, by Helen Reddy was popular. The correlation didn't dawn on me then, but as I prepared to write my perspective of this chapter, the Helen Reddy song continually popped into my thoughts:

"I am woman; hear me roar in numbers too big to ignore
and I know too much to go back and pretend.
Cause I've heard it all before, and I've been down there on the
floor.
No one's ever gonna keep me down again.
Oh yes, I am wise. But it's wisdom born of pain.
Yes, I've paid the price. But look how much I gained.
If I have to, I can do anything…

I am strong (strong)
I am invincible (invincible)
I am woman."

The embodiment of owning my presence, in conjunction with what my grandfather taught me, helped me realize that all energy can be shifted. From these two lessons, I created and led training regarding this shifting of energy to create a self-serving superpower.

Have you ever been in a room and felt someone walk in? They don't need to make a sound; their very presence changes the energy in the room. Many call it charisma; I call it the perfect example of the essence of energy transmutation. Those with this quality have learned to own their space. They have created an art of transmuting their energy to draw to them anyone in their path. Women who are phenomenal examples of this attitude are Sophia Loren, Dion Warwick, Hedy Lamarr, Eartha Kitt, Julie Andrews, Nichelle Nichols, Lucille Ball, Princess Diana, and Barbara Bush, to name a few. Each of these women created success by utilizing their magnetic energy, their comfort of being a woman, and knowing that attraction comes not from an outward physical appearance. The appeal of these women radiated from their essence of not apologizing for their sex, color, stature, social background, spouses' position, or public opinion. In my humble opinion, that is a superpower!

Another example of the transmutation of energy is personal magnetism. I speak about the power of personal magnetism in my training, *Amplify Your Magnetism.* Essentially, how to turn on and increase your personal charisma to attract what you want. Transmutation is beyond the physical aspect of attraction.

It is a shift of the physical to the mental capacity to attract what you desire in life. Through developing your magnetism and charisma, you purposefully activate your transmutation energy of attraction on a base level of awareness of self, ownership of who you are as an individual, and the energy you emit as a being of love, light, and goodness.

What does this involve? How can you, as a reader, activate this basic step of energy transmutation? The following are basic tools to amplify your magnetism which, in turn, switches your energy transmutation on. A song helps shift your mindset into a positively charged "can do" attractor. Have you ever been in a bad mood, then got into your car and heard your favorite upbeat song? Remember that moment. Were you able to stay in your bad mood? More than likely not. You begin to sing along, tap your feet, and forget your negative mindset.

Music is a powerful tool. Why is that? We are programmed from before birth to respond to a beat—our mother's heartbeat, the movement of her blood through her veins, and the muffled sounds from outside the serenity of her womb. So, when we are now outside the protection of our mother's body, our minds seek solid, familiar… music. The next is to do what the women I listed above managed to do: They owned their space and never apologized for being who they were.

Energy transmutation is not a physical shift. Transmutation is defined as "the action of changing or the state of being changed into another form." In this case, we are talking about the mental shift that occurs when a person no longer succumbs to the physical aspect of this human experience. Energy, by definition, cannot be destroyed; it can only be converted. The energy transmutation we speak of is a conversion of physical energy to be applied to fuel one's thoughts, creativity, and pursuits for success.

Let's look at the development of a relationship. New relationships are a perfect analogy for what occurs with energy transmutation. You meet someone, and there is an instant feeling of wanting. As you learn more about that person, you become obsessed; you get home and can't stop thinking of them, the sound of their voice, their smell, how they walk, their laugh, the way their hair falls across their face when they laugh —you know the pattern. You can see, smell, taste, and experience everything about them within your mind. You pursue them by being the best version of yourself. You pay attention to their every need. You court them by giving attention, spending quality time, and providing undivided attention. Together you dream of the life you will build together. If these dreams align, you create a life together.

This is energy transmutation: You focused all your energy on obtaining the relationship, courted another into the same end game, and it became a reality. The same conversion can happen with any object, goal, or achievement you truly desire. Focus on it. Dream of it. See, taste, smell, and live as you already know your end game. That focused excitement is the transfer of energy into reality.

The transformation of energy is most often used unintentionally. As we have discussed throughout this series of *The 13 Steps to Riches*, this energy must be focused on with intentionality. What do you want? Focus on it as if it were a relationship you long for and if you can channel that

excitement of your desire into an insatiable determination...
You will have achieved energy transmutation.

GETTING TO "YES" ENERGY!

It is basic human nature to want to succeed in life, to dream of a better future, or just to surpass those who came before them. Nobody wants to settle, whether it's in education, the job you currently have, or where you are living.

Instead of working towards improving your life financially so that you are able to one day obtain your dream job, house, car, or lifestyle, there are too many people who would rather do nothing out of fear of failure or making a mistake.

Everyone has their own special and unique gift that makes them who they are.

Unfortunately, they are held back by their fear of how they are perceived, so they would prefer to deny their gifts altogether. In order for someone to use their gifts to their fullest potential, they need to be recognized, nurtured, and protected.

Transformation in someone occurs when they overcome these negative thoughts and transmute the energy to achieve their desires. Napoleon Hill described this as transmutation.

In my book, *Yes! Energy*, I write that, "One of the most vicious threats, deep at the core of people's failure to properly exploit their God-given gifts, is a toxic little offender called... *perfection.*"

Perfect does not exist. There are no perfect people. There is no perfect world. While with the right energy and attitude, we can perceive everything to be perfect, trying to attain or achieve that state is a painful pursuit. Perfection is an ideal concept with no end in sight, preventing too many potential success stories from ever getting written.

Perfection does not allow for fast action or significant growth. Action is a gift. Using that gift means using energy to create, and that creation generates energy.

Part of the expense of doing business is the cost of wrong turns and mistakes. If a business or a person isn't willing to make mistakes and learn from those mistakes, there is no growth.

I try to preserve my energy by learning from the mistakes and imperfections of those who came before me. That's why I've had mentors and coaches since I was 17. I recommend always having a mentor or coach in your life. I believe in surrendering to a coach or teacher and letting that individual show me the way, instead of pursuing the route I think perfect for me.

Life lessons occur when learning from the mistakes and imperfections of those that came before us. You should always have a mentor or a coach in your life to help maneuver through life's obstacles. There are times when you will falter, the key is to get up, fix the problem, and learn from it. Those mistakes are there for you to learn from, so in the interim you will begin to make fewer and fewer mistakes.

In order to achieve the goals you want in life, you need to constantly change and grow. Perfectionists, however, do not like surrendering or making mistakes. Failing exposes their imperfection. In these cases, obstacles are avoided or denied, rather than confronted so they can learn from the experience and move on. Perfectionists do not pursue paths that contain obstacles, even though everything worthwhile has obstacles.

Too many live in this place of dreaming of success rather than taking a chance and seeing if it's possible. Worse, many do take a chance, fail, and crawl right back into the small place from which they came. You must fail a few times before you begin to succeed.

This stasis, this non-movement, is inaction. If action creates growth, then inaction shrinks a life.

Action is a gift. We are here to do and create. On the flip side, too many people get tangled up in a business that is not productive. People should physically embrace their imperfections. Instead, perfectionists strive to do every task as perfectly as possible but is the people who live their lives in abundance and fulfillment focus on their gifts of action and execution and cultivate an ability to perceive perfection even when everything is not quite perfect.

Our gifts are vulnerable to the attacks of outside and internal forces, which include, criticism, judgement, rejection, and indifference. The ability to take criticism well is a gift.

It is also a gift to offer criticism constructively.

If you are constructively criticized, you begin to learn what is helpful as you begin to live your life and what is not. If you are scolded in such a way that is traumatic, the lesson is less productive, and the gift of learning is damaged. This goes on throughout your lifetime, as we are always learning.

The ability to learn is one of our greatest skills, especially learning in a way that fuels our energy and builds an optimistic attitude by being able to take in good criticism and deflect the hurtful and mean criticism. In turn, we need to work on our capability to offer criticism to others that benefits them on a positive level.

Constructive criticism, given or received, should begin with an acknowledgment or a positive comment. I recommend the 5:1 ratio, or five positive comments for every one criticism. "Stay away from hurtful and get to helpful."

Putting yourself out there in the world sets you up for judgement. To combat hurtful remarks, you must use your gift of tolerance, for yourself and for others.

Think about the other person's perspective and try to understand if the judgment comes from an objective place.

Then you can decide how important it is for you to take on his or her judgment.

A big problem for many is that our affection for friends, partners, and family blinds us to their judgement. If you grew up in a codependent, dysfunctional family but don't even recognize that fact, then you're going to accept a lot of negative judgement that will deplete your energy and make you negative. Opening up your world to healthy people and enlightening experiences helps you find better sources of growth.

Getting rejected depletes your motivation to move forward. Getting rejected only means you move on and keep fighting. Getting rejected in either your personal or professional life feels like a personal attack. Hearing *no* is part of the process of getting to *Yes!* Make rejection part of the process of getting to where you want to be, but do not let rejection kill your gift.

Fortunately, you have the gift of fortitude. It feels bad to be rejected in one's personal or work life. All of it feels personal, but that feeling can be shifted with the right perspective. If you go out there and attempt to collect the *no's* in order to get to the *Yes!* then you make rejection part of the process.

Some might say that indifference is the cruelest attack on one's gifts. While criticism, judgment, and rejection are hurtful, they are at least active, if not negative, acknowledgments of one's gifts.

Indifference, though, is not reality for those who live in extreme energy. It only means that your gifts are being displayed in the wrong arena. The gifts of faith and certainty help us stay optimistic and energized.

When we truly recognize our gifts, we realize that these are not skills we created, but rather talents we were given and with which we were entrusted. If you truly believe in your mission and motives and are celebrating your gifts by using them, then no amount of indifference can get in your way.

If you drop your burdens, you can change the conversation to a new story. This progress, and that progress may lead to success. Plans rarely go exactly as you think they will, and success may not look the way you thought it would, but forward motion always puts you a step ahead of where you were and want to be.

Fear, guilt, shame, embarrassment, and small thinking are all adversaries that can attack our gifts and cause severe damage.

Fear being the biggest saboteur out there preys on what we are afraid of, which includes failure, rejection, trying something new, or our fear of wasted effort or potential disappointment.

Are you really afraid of failing or are you afraid of succeeding and the enormous responsibility of success that comes with it? Even if you don't succeed, or at least don't succeed in the way you wanted, you still did something. That experience of making an effort will make the next effort that much easier.

Moving forward always puts you a step ahead of where you were, even though plans rarely go exactly as you think they will, and success may not look the way you thought it would. Many people quit when they come upon those last few troubling obstacles. If you are fully exploiting your gifts, doing all you are capable of, and blasting into extreme energy, you can stay on track.

We feel selfish or unjustified in recognizing our gifts, so we play small. You cannot help anyone else until you have helped yourself, and if you're constrained or struggling in any way, then you don't have the freedom and energy to help others. By acknowledging your gifts, you empower yourself to create abundance for yourself and those you love.

As I've mentioned before, playing small is bad for you and those around you; it serves nothing and no one. When people engage scarcity thinking and believe that there is not enough, they fight and compete, and create fear and anxiety. If only you understood that there is more than enough for everyone, you would go get it with abandon.

Opportunity is about finding the right thing at the right time, not about numbers.

Confidence is a gift and truly believing in yourself and your gifts, can overcome guilt, shame, and embarrassment. Trust yourself and your abilities. This will inspire and uplift others to do the same.

Negative criticism and harsh judgment conditions you to thinking small while playing to lose. As with external criticism and judgment, our internal criticism and judgment can attack our gifts and be a detriment to our energy and optimism. These internal messages allow us to think that we are not good enough. Not good enough to accomplish more than the average person, not good enough to stand out from the crowd, not good enough to lead, an not even good enough to have a life that goes beyond basic survival.

There are many models of what abundance and excellence look like out there, and you can learn from, and become, one of them. Even these lives don't exemplify perfection, because there is no such thing. Life can be great without being perfect.

You can lead a life as fabulous as the one you perceive someone else is having without being perfect. The gift of unlimited human potential is yours as much as it is anyone else's.

If we as humans did not progress and grow, we would risk getting smaller and possibly evolving backward to a place of less ease and comfort, and more fear and despair. The gift of unlimited human potential must be nourished in order to attack small thinking. It begins with changing the conversation. Ask "Why?" Don't let something be just because it has always been that way. Too many people seek permission and follow others. Living your gifts is exploiting your gifts.

When you get a progressive, exciting, energizing idea in your head, consider how that new thought got delivered into your head in the first place. Those thoughts and ideas may be gifts. It's your duty to celebrate and exploit them.

We can have abundant, fun lives that are lived responsibly. That concept is the new conversation, and it begins by shifting our view of our place in this world.

Education cannot be passive. Children shouldn't receive anything, they should dig in actively and take their education.

Let's up the education ante by changing the system, helping children think creatively and expansively, tapping into all their skills, using even their latent and unique gifts.

There is too much focus on jobs, and the expectation that most people in this world is that they will go out and get a job, because they have to have one and that they deserve one.

Jobs do not encourage people to use their God-given talents and gifts. The United States was built on the entrepreneurial spirit to create.

Thanks to our freedom, our rights, and our liberties, no one has to buy into the economy and community into which they are born. Throughout history, people have created their own microeconomics where they find their talents and gifts, and then they have traded and leveraged those skills, as well as their resources.

Interdependent entrepreneurs is a party into which anyone can invite themselves. It requires recognizing that everything is not perfect. It requires seeing a demand and creating a supply, filling a niche or void, or empowering a chain by providing a stronger link.

This perspective of the economy and community changes the conversation and allows individuals to use their gifts.

Working hard and making a lot of money is an unreal correlation. There are plenty of people who have worked hard and gotten nowhere. On the other hand, there are those who have substantial wealth and didn't break a sweat. Those who know their gifts and use their strengths do not have to work as hard as those who depend on others and do the work they are told rather than the work at which they excel.

Planning to retire is planning to die. Retirement cannot be the endgame. i switch out the term retirement for Freedom Day –a time in your life when you can do what you want, when and with whom you want. Because you can.

There are so many areas in which we fail to live up to our gifts because we are afraid of being less than perfect.

If you are going to try to do a lot in this life, you are going to be wrong sometimes. In order to even attempt to change the conversation, you are going to have to allow yourself to try out new ideas and thoughts. Opening up a dialogue only to rationalize, defend, or justify closes down the avenues of growth.

Face it, when working to achieve your goals, you are going to look stupid sometimes. When you collect experiences that create the evidence you need in order to be confident, you are going to look stupid. Being vulnerable to saying and doing stupid things helps you strengthen your gifts. It builds your lightness, your humility, and your candor, and your empathy. The best gift, in these cases, is your sense of humor.

Life can be so much bigger and better if you are willing to let go of "perfect." Allow perfect to be perception, not reality, and every day of your life will be a happy one. Let go of perfect and you will let in a lot more excitement, energy, and optimism than you ever thought possible. This will attract others, and soon you will be part of a whole new team.

LORAL LANGEMEIER

Loral Langemeier is a money expert, sought-after speaker, entrepreneurial thought leader, and bestselling author of five books. Her goal is to change the conversation people have about money worldwide and empower people to become millionaires.

The CEO and Founder of Live Out Loud, Inc. – a multinational organization—Loral relentlessly and candidly shares her best advice without hesitation or apology. What sets her apart from other wealth experts is her innate ability to recognize and acknowledge the skills & talents of people, inspiring them to generate wealth.

She has created, nurtured, and perfected a 3-5 year strategy to make millions for the "Average Jill and Joe." To date, she and her team have served thousands of individuals worldwide and created hundreds of millionaires through wealth-building education keynotes, workshops, products, events, programs, and coaching services.

Loral is living proof that it makes no difference where you start in life; anyone can have the life of his or her dreams. Loral is a money expert, bestselling author, and Owner & CEO of Integrated Wealth Systems—A wealth coaching company.

Growing up on her family's farm in Nebraska, Loral learned the value of hard work, persistence and how to get things done even in the face of much opposition and criticism.

Loral began her career working for the Chevron Corporation right out of college. It was clear to her early on that there was more to life than cubicles and trading her time for dollars. Despite her own fears and persuasion from friends and family against it, Loral quit her job at Chevron to become an Executive Coach.

Virtually overnight, Loral quintupled her income as an Executive Coach, while working much less. With her newfound freedom of time and accumulation of wealth she founded Live Out Loud, Inc. As a single mother, Loral has since dedicated her life to helping men and women from all walks of life to become millionaires and have time to spend with their families.

Loral's straight talk and charming personality electrifies audiences and inspires powerful action from live stages and television programs ranging from CNN, CNBC, The Street TV, Fox News Channel, Fox Business Channel-America's Nightly Scoreboard, The Dr. Phil Show, and The View. She is a regular guest-host on The Circle in Australia and has been featured in articles in USA Today, The Wall Street Journal, The New York Times, Forbes Magazine and was the breakout star in the film The Secret.

CHAPTER 11
STAR IT!

When something is important, you must tell yourself, "Important/star it," so your brain will mark it for easy access when you need it.

Are you aware of the immense capacity we hold within us, particularly in the space between our ears? It's been calculated that the conscious mind processes approximately 40 bits of information per second. The subconscious mind can process 20,000,000 bits of information per second. We interact with the world with our conscious mind. We see a tree and think, "Oh, it's a tree." Then we determine what type of tree it is or whatnot. All the while, our subconscious mind is running through millions of bytes of data about the tree, i.e. height in relation to everything around the tree, species of trees we've seen before, color of the trunk along with the texture and pattern of that trunk.

Simultaneously, our subconscious is also calculating the multiple color variations of every leaf of that tree and the fluttering of each, whether an animal is in the tree or if a bird is flying by and at what rate the clouds are passing in relation to the angle in which the sunlight is reflecting upon the tree.

The next time you look at a tree, realize how much data your subconscious is really taking in. By the way, once you start assessing what your subconscious is taking in, the very thought causes a billion other data points for your subconscious to intake. The idea of thinking causing more thinking makes me smile. It brings to my mind (if we want to get very specific—the thought triggered my subconscious mind to remember) a scene from the movie, *Monty Python and the Holy Grail*. In it, one group is trying to tell another not to say a particular (albeit, common) word because it causes them great pain. When the offending group asks, "What word?" the first group keeps inadvertently saying it while trying not to, thus causing themselves harm. It's quite humorous to understand that what we focus on is what we bring about. Both groups were wanting to avoid the word but could not avoid it.

What do you not want to focus on? By saying you do not what to focus on it, all you do is continue to focus on what you don't want. It happens all the time. Focus on what you want, not what you don't want.

The immense capacity of the subconscious mind sounds like something out of a science fiction movie. Our brain has almost unlimited storage, but most of us have no idea of how to access it. Highly successful thought leaders have shared for generations that we must control the thoughts that enter our minds. The masters suggest that we can develop the skill to input intentionally and train our mind to retrieve what we need at will. We've discussed the prior concepts of the 13 Steps to Riches: Desire, Faith, Autosuggestion, Specialized Knowledge,

Imagination, Organized Planning, Decision, Persistence, Mastermind, and Transmutation. Each step requires the subconscious mind to be the big player to activate each of the other steps. The subconscious mind is the server mechanism that auto processes all experiences in our lives. There is nothing that we have sensed, whether it is seen, heard, smelled, tasted, touched, that hasn't been registered into the subconscious mind.

"The conscious mind is the editor, and the subconscious minds, the writer."
~ **Steve Martin**

I personally learned the power of our subconscious mind in 2014. I was involved in an auto accident that rendered me unable to move without assistance for over two years. I had obtained a traumatic injury to four areas of my brain. When I began my brain therapies, it became critical for me to not cloud my mind with negativity, violence, or anything that would cause my subconscious mind to process useless or harmful data.

We discovered, during my recovery, that if I watched a high stress or anxiety filled movie or listened to aggressive music, my thoughts, emotions and actions were more aggressive and I became more agitated. Watching nature videos and listening to ballads or classical music created a less agitated and happier me. Granted, I did not recognize the correlation. My family noticed and commented on what brought the best and worst out of me.

During that time, I had a sixteen-second memory. I was told by my husband that it was as if he was married to the girl from the movie, *50 First Dates* with Drew Barrymore. I had no recollection of the day prior. Every day was a new day for me. Slowly, I made progress with my cognition and recognition of people, places, and activities. My family was slowly and methodically creating new memories in my subconscious mind. The brain damage I had obtained presented a challenge and an opportunity. The challenge was that I lost most of my past experiences. The opportunity was to focus on creating new, pleasant memories in a fertile mind for growth.

The opportunity for growth was ideal. I listened to self-help lectures, joined the John Maxwell Team to hone my leadership skills, and met my mentor in the field of neuroscience and neuro-plasticity, Dr. Paul Scheele. I became highly aware of my ability to absorb information and internalize it quickly. It was as if the clutter within my subconscious mind was absent, and all the new behavior was readily accepted. I planted new belief systems, shed any of the past beliefs that would pop into my scattered memory, and reevaluate whether I wanted any of my old beliefs back. I chose what I allowed in.

With the auto accident and my four areas of traumatic brain injury, I was provided the biggest gift of all… a chance to start anew. This is why I have taken it upon myself to help others through their mental shifts into positivity. I have battled negative thoughts while locked inside my mind for over two years and for several years afterward as I was regrowing neuro-pathways in my mind. A few years into my recovery, I realized that the old thoughts of inadequacy where still in my mind. I simply chose to not let them materialize in my world or in my actions. Those negative thoughts did not serve the woman I visualized in the future. So, I let them go.

"Whatever we plant in our subconscious mind and nourish with repetition and emotion will one day become a reality."
~ Earl Nightingale

What you allow to remain in your subconscious will reveal itself in your conscious mind. I learned the direct way. There were days I would hear someone say, "Wow! You are doing so well. If I was going through what you have, I would be laying in the dark unable to move." Seriously, the next day, I would have a horrible headache, sit in the dark, and not want to move. My mind would add flair like nausea and vertigo. I let other people's thoughts invade my thoughts…my subconscious mind. We are that easily swayed even when we don't want to be swayed. That is why we must protect what our conscious mind is exposed to, so that we can protect our prized asset: our subconscious mind.

There's a quote about how you are the sum of the seven people you spend the most time with. It's not just the people. It also applies to what music or visuals you allow into your mind. Our subconscious is always learning. Let it learn and store the data that will build your character, create harmony in your world, and help you develop into the best version of yourself every day.

"My mission in life is not merely to survive, but to thrive and to do so with some, passion, some compassion, some humor and some style."
~ Maya Angelou

What do you want for your future? What thought processes do you have set on auto-play within your subconscious mind? Clean them up. Put what you want in order. Now, feed your mind your mantras, positive affirmations, and prayers daily. Then watch your world change for the better. What you focus on is what you draw toward yourself. Be sure to tell your brain "Important/star it," and watch what you want come to you.

EXCERPT BY DAME DORIA CORDOVA

THE SUBCONSCIOUS—THE GREATEST POWER

I am so honored to be part of this publication—to have the privilege of writing about the "greatest power" for any human being, the Subconscious, and to share what I've learned in nearly five decades of personally working on myself.

Once we understand the potential benefits and drawbacks of the Subconscious and we have established firewalls and self-mastery tools to deal with it under any adverse circumstance, our level of confidence, self-trust, and self-mastery goes through the roof!

I know that I can support you in having greater success, personal power, prosperity, health, peace, and joy. I can help you to have a life where you can live in the greatest experience of them all: Sufficiency!

The Subconscious mind has been a topic of fascination and debate for centuries. It is widely known that our Subconscious thoughts and emotions play a significant role in shaping our decisions and relationships, especially in the business world… Everywhere we look!

Bottom line: The Subconscious has a huge influence on our lives. Allow me to offer practical guidance on overcoming these pitfalls, fostering greater conscious awareness, and enhancing the overall quality of important decisions.

To give you a little context as to why I have "earned the right" to speak about this subject, let me share a bit about my life. Through a series of wondrous circumstances that I consciously never imagined, I became part of the team of pioneers of the entrepreneurial, experiential, transformational training industry in the late 1970s which now permeates the industry globally. This field, of course, supports people around the world to clear their Subconscious and reach the life of their dreams.

Everyone's life is affected by Generalized Principles. A Generalized Principle is always true. These are principles proven by science and physics. Whether we believe in them or not, they exist. One Generalized Principle is **gravity**; another is **leverage**; and one not so well-known but equally powerful is **precession**. Precession is the physics term for ripple effects. They are always present.

The synergy that can be created when we understand how powerfully the Subconscious affects our thoughts, behaviors, feelings, and actions, and learn to manage it, is extraordinary.

At the young age of 26, through a spiritual awakening, and having attended one of the first (and most successful) human potential trainings, EST, I was blessed to learn at the time that if I couldn't have control over my circumstances (I had experienced the tremendous loss of my beloved, two miscarriages, and a dozen friends), at least I could have control of my consciousness.

I finally had a glimpse that I could have a life that could work for me with much less fear, anxiety, and stress… The possibilities were heavenly! I knew I could be financially successful. I just didn't know that I could also be personally happy and live a purpose-driven life.

Once I started putting my attention on clearing my Subconscious of negative programming, my life pivoted to what eventually led me to create the results that are evident today.

In the 1970s, there wasn't as much research as we have now. We now know that self-mastery work, exercise, breathing, healthy foods, a focus on adding value to others, being loving and kind, having integrity, and committing our lives to the betterment of humanity can bring us true happiness and joy.

As a Latina woman having accomplished the "American dream," I know that it had much to do with the values that were taught to me by my mother, auntie, grandmother, and other amazing family members that led my thinking.

And then there was the Subconscious…

I had to overcome strong beliefs, thoughts, and decisions that I had made because of my environment, as I had been literally "brainwashed" in traditional schools (as had everyone else). I had to learn Financial Literacy on my own by attending programs like the Burklyn Business School (which evolved to what I own today, the Excellerated Business School) and many programs taught by experts outside of traditional education.

I had to clear Subconscious blocks to achieve the level of success that I knew I had in me, and thank God, I realized that I actually had to raise my "deservability" level in order to allow more success, in every area of my life.

How did I do that? First, I am eternally thankful to Sondra Ray, one of the original metaphysicians who influenced many of the leaders in the industry, including myself. When I discovered that I wanted to commit myself to the betterment of humanity and attended the first business school for entrepreneurs of its kind that I mentioned earlier, all these negative thoughts began to literally spurt from my Subconscious. I found myself fighting beliefs that I literally didn't know I had.

She then introduced me to the *"Magical Exercises"* (a title that emerged after decades of personally using them, as many other leaders in our industry). I had to clear my Subconscious of the beliefs about money, business, and success that I had learned from my parents, family, school, church, books, movies, the environment—essentially, the world!

Most of humanity is programmed to believe that we live in a world of scarcity—even though the Malthusian theory of economics (the work of governments is to manage scarce resources) was proven obsolete in the early 1970s. Think about that… That was over 50 years ago! It was proven then that the world had enough resources to feed everyone, to house everyone.

The systems and tools were there to share energy sources for the world to have electricity, which is essential to eradicating poverty and hunger. We actually live in a world that has enough, yet sufficiency is one of the most fleeting experiences for so many!

If you don't believe that, your Subconscious is hard at work. And here's where the daily, moment-to-moment discipline comes into play: take three deep breaths. Feel the reaction, question what is being activated, and decide if (whatever you are feeling) is something that is worth working on so that you are the CEO of your life, and the captain of your ship. This will help you clearly and soberly make decisions that will empower you to have a successful life.

Recognize when you are in reaction. Take three deep breaths and come back to center. Do the work and find that inner family that can lead you to have more courage, more clarity, and more certainty than that which you choose, which will lead you to a better life.

I learned this very young: Just because I don't believe something, doesn't mean that it isn't true. Your beliefs will taint your reality, so that you will find the evidence necessary to make those beliefs true. You can actually see it in the division that has been created in the world today around medicine, science, and technology.

Who is running the show, you or your Subconscious? Are you aware of the beliefs that you have about the subject that you are tackling today? Do you have the correct information, facts, and what has worked in that situation? Are you willing to learn from other people's mistakes? Or are you the type that will spend the rest of your life having the same "learning experiences" (mistakes), hoping for a different outcome?

Do the *Magical Exercises* that have made a huge difference to so many who have done them. You can find them in our www.FridaysWithDoria.com global platform under *Resources*. Clear your Subconscious and do the daily work to create a reality that empowers you, that allows you to find the information, tools, and techniques that have worked for tens of millions to have a successful business, or organization (for-profit or non-profit).

Study those who have created extraordinary results in the area that you are interested in, or already have success in. Remember, there are **three stages of money: making it, keeping it, and growing it.** What stage are you in? Each stage requires for your Subconscious to have empowering beliefs every step of the way. It's the greatest power, after all.

If your Subconscious is running amok with beliefs that you have collected unchecked, you will have chaos. If you are aware of them and are CONSCIOUSLY working on them, you will have power.

"It is the Way," as they say in the *Mandalorian – Star Wars* offshoot.

Consciously increase your self-awareness. Developing a deeper understanding of your emotions, thoughts, and biases can help you recognize when they might be influencing your decision-making. Mindfulness meditation, journaling, and self-reflection exercises such as the *Magical Exercises* are effective ways to cultivate self-awareness.

I personally have practiced Transcendental Meditation (TM) for 14 years without fail. It has been one of my greatest disciplines, and here's why.

Once you begin to have self-mastery, you will find that your intuition (gut feeling) will become more prevalent... Your ability to process new information and experiences will lead you to insights that may not be immediately apparent through logical analysis. Intuition can be a valuable tool in making quick decisions or identifying potential opportunities and risks. My ability to make decisions has sped up and improved.

Your emotional intelligence will increase exponentially. You will find that certain situations that used to trigger you no longer do. Learn to manage your emotions effectively. Acknowledge and validate your emotions but avoid letting them dictate your decisions. Techniques such as emotional intelligence training, stress management, and seeking feedback from trusted mentors, colleagues, and friends can help you regulate your emotions and make more balanced decisions.

You will excel at identifying patterns and connections between seemingly unrelated pieces of information, which can lead to innovative ideas and solutions. You will have enhanced creativity. Many creative insights and ideas arise from the subconscious mind, often when we least expect them. This can lead to breakthroughs in problem-solving and the development of new products or strategies.

I recommend that you create environments that foster creativity in your business, organization, and family! Encourage brainstorming sessions, open discussions, and collaboration within your teams/family to stimulate the Subconscious mind and generate innovative ideas. Providing a safe space for experimentation and risk-taking can lead to breakthroughs in problem-solving.

Remember, the Subconscious mind wields significant influence over our business decisions and relationships. By understanding its origins and recognizing its potential benefits and drawbacks, we can develop strategies to harness its power and not only make better-informed decisions, we can also design our lives so that we actualize our most cherished heart's desires!

May the Force Be with You!

DAME DORIA (DC) CORDOVA, PHD (HON.)

Dame Doria Cordova owns *Excellerated Business Schools® for Entrepreneurs* and *Money & You®*, a global organization that has over 165,000 participants for the past 42 years from over 85 countries, especially from Asia Pacific and the Americas. The programs are taught in English, Chinese, and Japanese–soon expanding to Tamil, Hindi, and other Indian languages–plus, Spanish, Bahasa, and more… Many of today's wealth and business leaders have attended the *Money & You* program and transformed the way they teach and run their organizations.

Through these graduates, including her business partnership of 9 years in the 80's and '90's with Robert T. Kiyosaki of *Rich Dad/Poor Dad* fame, Dame Cordova's work has touched the lives of millions all over the world. The essence of her work is to not only focus on the bottom line and profits but also to offer products and services that add value to humanity.

She is the only Latin woman that was part of the group of pioneers, led by Marshall Thurber and Bobbi DePorter of **_www.Supercamp.com_**, that began the development of the transformational, experiential, entrepreneurial training industry. She inherited the work over 36 years ago which has now expanded to what it's today through countless partners, associates, teams, graduates and the support of many.

Along with Robert Kiyosaki, of the *Rich Dad/Poor Dad* series, in 1985 they opened that industry in Australia, New Zealand and later Singapore. Subsequently, along with new partners, the Malaysia, Taiwan, Hong Kong, China, Indonesia, India, Thailand, Philippines, Cambodia and other markets have been opened. Their larger market is in the Chinese language—having been in China for 19 years. Dr. Willson Lin and his team have put the programs "on the map". Her latest expansion of the work is the English ***Global Excellerated Business School for Entrepreneurs***. This global gathering of global social entrepreneurs will be held in Port Douglas, North Queensland, Australia on November 6 – 14, 2021

CHAPTER 12
MUSCLE MEMORY

"The brain is like a muscle. When it is in use, we feel very good."
~ Carl Sagan

I have learned that when the mind is idle, it loses track of what it is meant to do. After six months of the 2020 COVID-19 pandemic lockdown, many people witnessed or experienced this phenomena firsthand. Those who were quarantined in solitude experienced it faster. What happened? Once the novelty of the extended vacation wore off and we realized we needed personal interactions, we sought distractions from our long, lonely days. Moments blurred into each other. We lost track of minutes, hours, and days. Our time was consumed by surfing the internet, binging shows, stress eating, and other unhealthy habits. Our minds and bodies became idle.

"An idle mind is the devil's playground."
~ Philippians 4:8

The mind is like a muscle. When you stop using it, it begins to atrophy. This happened around the world. We congruently experienced a medical pandemic which set off a domino effect of depression, despair, obesity, loss of jobs and, in turn, the atrophy of minds. For those who were wishing for some time off, the global shutdown was a wish granted. From such tales as Aladdin and the Magic Lamp from The Arabian Nights bedtime stories, we learned lessons like, "Be careful what you wish for," and, "You are greater than your situation."

In this case, some discovered new skills, some found other outlets for creativity, and online communities were created. In all the chaos and uncertainty, good did occur. Unfortunately, many never came out of the downward spiral. Some became accustomed to not moving or working. They allowed their apathy to take a grip on their mindset and they have become less of a person from the experience.

I witnessed this decay of society during hundreds of online community calls, trainings, and keynote addresses I have done throughout the pandemic and the years afterward. The decline in hope and the increase of apathy has been significant among many.

I had seen this occur before in my life personally. When I was a military spouse, I moved with my active-duty husband every four years. I had great difficulty obtaining a job with so many frequent moves. Once we had children, the opportunity to work became even more difficult since my husband deployed for weeks at a time, which often left me as a single parent in a foreign county. There were times when I would find myself tearing up or crying from the loss of myself. Every waking moment was scheduled around our young children.

My mind, which was accustomed to high levels of activity, including reading and adult interaction, was not being fed. I felt as if I was losing my mind. I began to dream scenarios that seemed so real that when my husband would return from a deployment, I would accuse him of things that never happened. My mind lost connection to reality. My husband and I discussed my delusional state. He shared with me that he saw the same occur with his mother. She was a teacher but over the summer, she would get silly. His theory, I agreed, was that we were both highly intelligent women and when we had nothing to stimulate our brains, we lost touch with reality. It made sense.

How, as a stay-at-home mother, could I keep my mind active while caring for our young children? I became creative with our days: Outings to museums and historical locations, play dates, teaching our children science, learning advanced baking skills and the like improved my brain function back to normal. Bonus, our children learned at an accelerated rate.

As our children became more independent, my interest gravitated to returning to college, taking courses on cooking or the learning the language of the country we lived. Now that our children are adults, I have expanded my brain repertoire. During the two-plus year setback I experienced in 2014 with my traumatic brain injury, I had to relearn all everyday skills. I believe my neuropathways were more receptive to regrowth because I had challenged my brain for most of my adult life with everything I mentioned above along with word searches, crosswords and puzzles. The brain is like a muscle. Once I began to challenge it, my brain remembered how to flex, much like muscle memory.

If we are fortunate, we will reach our retirement years. You have probably seen your parents, a family member, or friend retire. Perhaps, you have reached your retirement? I challenge you to keep your mind and body active. It is important that we keep exercising that "muscle" between our ears every day of our lives.

Upon retirement, keep challenging your mind with new experiences. If you can't travel, visit places within your area. Be a tourist in your town. Play games. Meet new people. Join a mastermind or a group that piques your interest. Every day, complete a word or number puzzle. Keep your mind active and you will reap the benefits of remaining cognitive longer. An active mind has been proven to reduce the onset of Alzheimer's Disease.

Outside of your job, how do you keep your mind actively creating? Add habits to your routine that challenge your mind. Build a strong foundation by adding mental resiliency exercises into your life. The best time to work on increasing your mental acuity is before you start to lose it.

We must remember the lesson that we are greater than our situation or circumstances. Regardless of what you are experiencing, we each have a choice to remain where we are or move through. It is a mindset embraced by those who succeed consistently: Use your mind and your intuition to find your own way through difficult times and keep moving regardless of the pace or whether you know how.

You probably noticed I mentioned intuition as a factor to success. It is quite a major factor in those who embody the Think and Grow Rich mentality. The unconscious mind has been studied and part of Eastern religions for centuries. The Western world has recently begun to embrace its importance and recognize that there is more to our minds than what is easily measured. The unconscious mind is referred to as an inner knowing or intuition.

Have you experience the phenomena where a particular person appears in your dreams or you feel the need to reach out to them? Once you do, you discover they were experiencing a stressor and needed you. Perhaps you've had a gut feeling that you want to avoid someone or to take another route to your destination? If you haven't had this kind of experience, perhaps you've heard of one?

The brain is incredible. I believe it has more capabilities than we are willing to admit and that these intuitive feelings or nudges occur constantly within our lives. We don't notice them because our minds are preoccupied with the constant bombardment of information through our electronic devices and busy lives.

I encourage you to find moments of quiet time in your day. Listen for the quiet voice. Your intuition is speaking. Just like your body, your subconscious mind, needs to be exercised in order to work better. Exercise of the subconscious mind is done with meditation. Turn off your mind to allow your subconscious to play a more active role in your life, by creating an opportunity to see beyond what your conscious mind can visualize.

Make it a practice to exercise your brain's capabilities not only through challenging the logical conscious mind, but also the unconscious mind. If you have not experienced meditation, seek meditation guidance online or join a group that will teach you how to quiet your mind. Once you learn the basics, you can create a practice to do it daily.

EXCERPT BY JOHN ASSARAF

YOUR BRAIN & SELF-LIMITING BELIEFS

THE GOOD, THE BAD, & THE UGLY

If no one had told you otherwise, would you believe that the Earth was flat, the stars were celestial beings, and beyond the horizon, the sea dropped off into oblivion?

If you're like most modern people, you have other ideas in mind.

A spherical Earth spins on an axis; the planets revolve around the Sun. Stars aren't gods of fire—they're luminous spheroids of plasma. If a crowd of people were to try to convince you otherwise, you'd have centuries of scientific evidence to prove them wrong.

But what if, when you woke up each morning, you assumed that nothing much existed beyond *your* horizon?

What if every time you saw yourself in the mirror, your reflection echoed back: "You're neither smart nor spectacular enough to succeed," "You're too unlucky to ever be loved"?

Would you let those beliefs prevent you from setting sail to see what truly lies on your horizon?

TAKE 'EM TO TASK

Sadly, there's no peer-review in your head to fact check any ideas you may have of yourself. There's no objective eye in your prefrontal cortex to test the validity of the hypotheses you've formed about your life, the universe, and everything.

It's all too easy to turn conjectures into conclusions. Theories into dogma. Impressions into judgments.

A statement like "I'm worthless," "I'm unlovable," or "I'm doomed to failure" might sound harmless if you say it once. But words have a way of persuading even unbelievers you repeat them often enough. You may find yourself cherry-picking memories from your personal history to prove to yourself that the beliefs you hold in the present are true.

Call it negative self-talk. Self-flagellation. The devil on your shoulder. None of us have escaped the clutches of self-limiting beliefs. They creep up when we're about to step out of our comfort zone. They may pull us into cowardice when we feel brave enough to follow a dream. They often lurk below the field of awareness, which makes them even more insidious. Scientists have been trained to scrutinize any theory they have about the universe.

Isn't it time to take your negative self-talk to task?

WHAT THE BLEEP'S BEHIND A BELIEF?

What goes on in your brain when you believe—in a benevolent creator of the universe, in life-after-death, or in damnation for that matter? Why, from the perspective of the evolution of cognition, do human beings form belief systems—like religion—in the first place?

Social scientists ask why cultures transmit systems of belief: Why do native Polynesians see spirits in the waves and Catholics feel certain of the Holy Trinity? Biologists see beliefs as traits of evolution: Which social and emotional interactions have led to their formation?

To neuroscientists, beliefs run deeper than the culture or the social and environmental contexts. They represent complex brain-based phenomena that form the basis of all social exchanges and moral intuitions.

THE GOOD

When you trust in the goodness of your neighbors, it enables you to participate in community life, and to form healthy social bonds. Without community, you might find it difficult to thrive, let alone survive, in the world. Unless your neighbors prove otherwise, it's healthy for your brain to believe that they're decent people.

Moreover, a belief in karma, or "what goes around comes around," also encourages neighbors to act ethically towards each other. Codes of behavior, at their best, help people to live in relative peace.

THE BAD

Beliefs also offer people a way to cope when difficult things happen in life. They help humans to accept misfortune. If you grow up with a cat, and that cat gets hit by a bus, it's comforting to believe in an animal heaven. When a volcano erupts, a belief in a just but fiery god can help people to make sense of devastation.

THE UGLY

Along the same lines, when you say to yourself, "I'm unworthy," your brain might be looking for an easy way to make sense of personal misfortune. Although the human brain is a complex and intricately fascinating organ—it's also lazy. If your brain can operate with minimal effort, it will. Thinking that you're unworthy of love may be the quickest pathway your brain has found to protect you from the losses and disappointments inherent in intimate human relationships.

WHERE IN THE BRAIN IS BELIEF?

Some neuroscientists hypothesize that specific patterns of brain activity play different roles in the art of believing. Some beliefs engage posterior regions of the brain while others engage areas involved in abstract reasoning. Whenever you believe anything about yourself—whether it's "I'm a mess" or "I'm the best thing since sliced bread," you engage brain networks involved in memory retrieval and imagery.

The default mode network, or what some researchers call "the imagination network," plays a central role in formulating and maintaining beliefs about who you think you are. It's the network that governs all your autobiographical memories. It daydreams about who you might have been in the past and who you think you might be in the future.

The more you recall ideas and feelings about yourself, the stronger the neural pathways that carry those memories will get. That process is what forms your self-concept; it's what builds your identity. Freud referred to the whole thing as the "ego."

Whatever you call it, a consistent belief in who you are as a person also has an evolutionary purpose. Without a stable sense of self, life would be a helluva thing to navigate.

AYE, THERE'S THE RUB

Now, this may be hard to believe—but every belief you have about yourself is "self-limiting."

Do you believe that you are good? Bad? Ugly?

Whatever you believe and however you believe it, you're putting limits around who you truly are. As Shakespeare's

Hamlet says in Act 2, Scene 2: "There is nothing either good or bad, but thinking makes it so."

If you think you are a "good" person, that belief may be preventing you from appreciating the full spectrum of your personality. Believing in your unassailable goodness can lead to all forms of denial. But if you believe yourself to be a "bad" person, is it any better?

WHAT'S THE SOLUTION: INNERCISE!

Train your brain to keep those self-limiting beliefs from running wild and unverified in your mind. Just as you wouldn't drink milk past its due date, don't swallow ideas about yourself just because they're sitting on the front shelf of your brain!

You exercise your leg muscles when you walk an extra mile. Now walk an extra mile in your mind. Innercise the "muscles" (or synapses) that form your neural pathways, so they remain agile, responsive, and awake.

Expand your potential for deeper levels of awareness. Whenever your default mode network starts stirring up beliefs about who you think you are, notice those beliefs for what they are.

But first, take a moment and notice the pattern of your breathing. Is it quick? Soft? Labored?

Whatever you're experiencing, let go of any judgment.

Notice your physical body in the present. If it helps, gently caress the palms of your hands. Experience pleasure, without judgment, blame, shame, guilt, or justification, in this moment. Let go of any beliefs of who you think you might be right now. If beliefs arise, just notice them dispassionately.

When you feel relaxed and steady in your body and mind, tap into your wise inner voice (or your expert innerciser if you prefer).

Ask your expert innerciser: What beliefs do I harbor about myself that are reigning in my true self? Are any of my beliefs holding me back from living fully? Are any of my ideas about who I am inhibiting me from meeting my potential? From reaching my goals?

Write down those beliefs.

Now read them back. Slowly. Calmly.

Recognize that whatever you're reading is something you've taken part in constructing. It's all fabrication. And if it's limiting you now, you have the power to let the story go.

When you achieve a little distance from those self-limiting beliefs, recognize and relish in having freedom from them. The more you do this, the more it will become a habit and the more natural it will feel to sit in the driver's seat in front of an open road.

In this space of freedom, it's your call. It's your turn. Hands on the wheel.

Choose to believe something new about yourself. Go down a different road. Play a different part in your own life. Believe in your self-worth, your beauty, your potential. Whatever you wish.

Do you believe that you can meet your financial goals this year? Why not? What's holding you back? Is it something tangible? Can you name the limitations you're putting on your financial freedom? Write those barriers down and see them for what they are.

Do the same for any goal you may have, whether it's love or work or travel. Check in next week as we tackle the neuroscience of goal setting and achievement.

Now that you know a little bit more about what self-limiting beliefs are, isn't it easier to just sail past them?

JOHN ASSARAF

John Assaraf, *"The Brain Whisperer,"* is one of the leading high-performance success coaches in the world. He is a behavioral neuroscience researcher who has appeared numerous times on Larry King Live, Anderson Cooper, and The Ellen DeGeneres Show.

As CEO and co-founder, he grew Re/Max of Indiana from a startup to 85 offices and 1200 sales associates who sold over $4 billion a year.

John was also one of the founders of Bamboo/IPIX, which went public on NASDAQ with a market cap of $2.5 billion.

John has written four books, including two New York Times bestsellers, that have been translated into 35 languages. He is the creator of the "Innercise" movement and has been featured in 11 movies, including the blockbuster hit *The Secret* and *Quest For Success* with Richard Branson and the Dalai Lama.

He lives in San Diego with his wife and two sons. In addition to being a vegan, meditator, an avid skier, and ocean lover, he loves traveling the world and making some of the tastiest hot sauces using some of the hottest peppers on the planet.

Today, he is CEO of MyNeuroGym.com, a neuroscience-based company, dedicated to helping individuals strengthen their mindset, so they achieve their goals and dreams... faster and easier than ever before.

CHAPTER 13

A DUCK IS A DUCK… OR IS IT?

The subconscious mind is the most powerful tool in your arsenal to achieve success. We have read throughout the series of 13 Steps to Riches, based on the Think and Grow Rich by Napoleon Hill, that behind each of the 12 prior steps, success requires the ability to master one's mind. Our thoughts, beliefs, and emotions are fueled by the subconscious mind. It is imperative that we make a conscious effort to listen and obtain guidance from our subconscious. Without this step, the manifesting of the intangible into the tangible is lost. The manifestation is accomplished through the use of imagination, visualization, auto-suggestion, and affirmations. We need our conscious mind to align with our subconscious mind to transform our dreams into reality. Without the subconscious, our goals are merely dreams.

Each of us has a sixth sense. At what level of awareness we work, this sixth sense varies. It helps us make decisions very quickly based on our past experiences. As a professional speaker, thought leader, author, and entertainer, I run in circles of individuals who persistently seek self-improvement. We often speak about, "What does your gut say?" or "What is your first instinct reaction?" It never occurred to me that someone would not think in terms of seeking self-improvement. This is why I was caught off guard when a woman approached me to say she had no idea what I was speaking about. I mentioned "gut instinct" and "intuition" during my talk on stage. She was quite a logical woman. She informed me that she doesn't make decisions based on feelings; rather, she uses facts. This "woo hoo" adaption of making decisions off indigestion troubled her. We talked for quite a while and she explained her process of making decisions. She mentioned how she takes all the data she can collect into account to make a decision. I said, "That is an educated guess. This is your intuition!" Her face lit up, knowing that she did have her version of "gut feelings." We discussed further as I compared her logic to how "gut feelings" are a subconscious assessment of everything she had ever learned, heard, witnessed, experienced, read, etc. In essence, no one is truly using an emotional trigger; we are accessing our subconscious mind at such a high rate that we don't recognize the process as a checklist of what we have come to know but rather a quick, united response to all that our subconscious has compiled. That explanation helped both of us that day.

As I further pondered the power of the unconscious mind, I realized that although it allows us to make decisions quickly, they are not always the right ones. Sometimes, our past, especially if it is traumatic, can have an oversized effect on us. I have a perfect example of my "gut feeling" negatively affecting my logical thoughts. About two months into the COVID-19 lockdown, I used the worldwide lockdown to evaluate my life and the trajectory of my career as a professional speaker in a world without live conferences. Like many of us, I was connecting with people on social media, but I needed human contact. I sought communities to feed my soul and mind. As I was browsing through a social media site, I saw a face pop-up as a suggested friend. I dismissed him because I had met him in the past, and there was something about his demeanor that didn't sit well with me. He had never done anything to me, but my "gut" told me to stay away. It finally hit me; he reminded me of someone who had hurt me in the past. My subconscious mind was saying, "If it looks like a duck, sounds like a duck, it's probably a duck." Basically, I prejudged this man as being exactly like the person who hurt me. I would run into him at local networking meetings and quietly walk away. I never initiated or followed through on any interaction. In my mind, he was a "duck". I chose to ignore his existence. Stuck in my home with only online social media, this man kept showing up in my feed. It was obnoxious how often, despite my attempts to ignore him, social media continued to suggest him as a connection. Then, I began to see his posts through my friend's comments. What in the world is going on?

I continued to ignore this man as I persisted in my self-discovery work. I had successfully battled all my phobias and insecurities, with the exception of one, the man who reminded me of someone who hurt me. That day, I went onto my computer, and again, his face popped up. Logic told me that I conquered all the other roadblocks in my life, and I will hopefully never meet the person who hurt me again. The best way to beat this fear was to approach it directly. That faithful morning, I wrestled with my fears to simply send a connection request to this man I didn't care to know. He immediately accepted. My insides turned. What had I done? I may have just allowed my greatest fear back into my life. I watched his profile for a week. I scanned his old posts. Nothing vulgar. Nothing mean. Not anything like I expected him to be. We had hundreds of mutual friends. How bad can he be? My imagination had made him an older version of the person I knew from college. I expected to connect virtually with him and see validation of all my fears, but I didn't see any negative evidence. I realized that I was still afraid. To overcome this fear, I must do something more. I needed to speak to him. I sent him a private message to start a conversation. We saw humor in the same things. We both had a very practical view of all the chaos that was surrounding the world during the worldwide lockdown. Could I be that wrong about a person? I truly pride myself on my gut instincts. I needed to take a bolder step. I invited myself over to his front porch for a beer. Keep in mind, this is during the full COVID-19 lockdown with all the social distancing. I breached two stomach-wrenching dangers at once: 1) COVID and 2) him.

As I walked up to his porch, he had a selection of beers for me to choose from. We sat socially distanced on his porch, drinking beers as we had discussion after discussion. He was nothing like my imagination created him to be. He was a good-humored man with deep thoughts. Even when we disagreed, it was fun to play verbal volleyball with him. As the weeks passed, our chairs moved closer together. He became a good friend. One day, I decided to tell him why I avoided him for the 18 years prior. He was horrified that he had caused me so much anxiety. I apologized for judging him by his look, mannerisms, voice and choice of cars. His personality and mind is nothing of what I feared. Years have now passed. We have created a podcast together called Denim and Pearls - Business casual with pearls of wisdom from the porch… where our friendship started.

My lessons learned through the development of our friendship:

1.   My "gut instinct"/ subconscious mind was marred by my past. I had a list of physical qualities in my mind that I had learned were dangerous. My conscious mind kept seeing him over the years, but I subconsciously avoided him.
2.   I had to step toward what I irrationally feared.
3.   Don't judge a book by its cover.

If I allowed my subconscious mind to rationally keep me hostage in fear, I would have never met Brian Swanson. He has helped me numerous times through his ability to see life through a different lens. My conscious mind was so quiet. It nudged me gradually to see past what my subconscious refused to permit. My request to you is to challenge your beliefs every once in a while. Is there someone you keep running into that you are weary of for no reason to speak with? Step out of your comfort zone. Start a conversation. You never know what your marred subconsciousness is keeping you from discovering. Perhaps you are missing out on your next level of friendship. It could also be affecting your business. Perhaps you are avoiding changes, people, or potentials based on a previous bad experience. Logic it out and move on.

"Your friends will know you better in the first minute you meet than your acquaintances will know you in a thousand years."

~ Richard Bach

EXCERPT BY KEVIN HARRINGTON

MASTERING INTUITIVE DECISION-MAKING

For over forty years, I've built, invested in, and scaled businesses worldwide. You might know me from the television show, *Shark Tank,* or perhaps from my role in creating the modern infomercial. Through these ventures and countless others, I've refined my decision-making process to the point where I can often rely on a feeling—an instinctual sense—to guide me in the split second it takes to decide whether an opportunity is worth pursuing. That instinct is what Napoleon Hill calls the "sixth sense" in *Think and Grow Rich.* It's not something I had when I first started, but over the years, I've developed this ability, this "entrepreneurial radar," through trial, error, and intentional practice.

The sixth sense isn't a mystical force; it's the culmination of knowledge, experience, and quick analysis—the subconscious mind applying what you know and feel in the moment. It's an edge; when you're in business, that edge can mean the difference between a missed opportunity and a multimillion-dollar success. This is the most challenging trait for people to learn and obtain because it involves a gut feeling and developing the sense through all of the other steps in this process.

Today, I'll share how I developed my sixth sense in business, the process I use to make rapid, accurate decisions, and the key lessons I've learned that you can apply in your own journey toward mastering intuitive decision-making.

DEVELOPING THE SIXTH SENSE

When I was starting out as a young entrepreneur in the 1980s, I didn't have what you'd call a sixth sense. I was just trying to get a foothold in the industry. My journey began with a $25,000 investment in Quantum International, which eventually became a $500-million-a-year business listed on the New York Stock Exchange. That success didn't happen overnight, nor did my sense for evaluating risk and opportunity. But with time and experience, I found myself developing a deeper, almost automatic intuition.

In business, I have been pitched thousands upon thousands of ideas. In fact, over a decade after *Shark Tank*, I still receive about a thousand pitches a month. This is where my sixth sense has truly been refined. On *Shark Tank*, contestants had just three minutes to sell their concept, and I had three minutes to decide if I wanted to invest potentially millions of dollars. There wasn't time for in-depth due diligence. I had to rely on my gut and make fast decisions, which were often based on what I've come to know as my sixth sense.

THE FOUNDATION: THE TEN-STEP PROCESS

Early in my career, I realized that a clear set of criteria could bolster my intuition. So, I began documenting the qualities I looked for in a potential product or business idea. Over time, I identified ten core factors that I could quickly evaluate. These were things like market potential, the uniqueness of the solution, scalability, and the ability to reach a mass audience. I would go down this list mentally, sometimes even subconsciously, checking off points as I listened to a pitch.

For instance, in a pitch, I look for a clear "tease" or problem that catches attention immediately. Then, there's the "please," where the solution is presented, showing how this product can meet a real need or deliver value. Finally, there's the "seize," where the offer becomes irresistible. If I could see these elements in a pitch and if it ticked enough of my ten boxes, that's when I knew I had something.

AN EXAMPLE OF THE SIXTH SENSE IN ACTION: THE GREAT WOK OF CHINA

One of the best examples of my sixth sense in action is the story of the Chinese wok. About 35 years ago, I took my team to a trade show to scout potential products. We divided up the convention floor, and after a few hours, my team returned empty-handed, thinking the show had been a dud. But I'd found something—a hand-hammered wok made in mainland

China. It was unique, with ridges that cooked food differently and more efficiently.

My team was skeptical; they couldn't see the potential. "You can get a wok for $10 at Walmart," they said. But they didn't listen to the story behind it. This was no ordinary wok—it was authentic, hand-hammered in a way that brought out the best flavors in the food. I trusted my gut, invested in it, and spent $3,500 to create an infomercial. That product, marketed as "The Great Wok of China," went on to make $250 million in sales. This was my sixth sense at work, and it was only possible because I was open to seeing the opportunity where others saw none.

LEARNING FROM EXPERIENCE

Think of it as a muscle that gets stronger over time. The more pitches I heard, the more products I evaluated, the sharper my instincts became. And the more I documented what worked and what didn't, the more I learned to trust my own judgment. This is why I encourage entrepreneurs to pay attention to the signals, document what they learn, and refine their approach.

Over time, I learned to dig deeper, read between the lines, and anticipate potential roadblocks. Sometimes, it's not just about what the person says but how they say it. Are they confident? Are they passionate? Do they believe in what they're selling? These intangible factors contribute to that sixth sense, helping me quickly assess whether something is worth my time and investment.

TRUSTING YOUR GUT, BUT BACKING IT WITH RESEARCH

Having a sixth sense is essential, but so is balancing it with a dose of reality. Even with solid instincts, I never make decisions based on feeling alone. It's always backed by research and quick verification whenever possible. Early in my career, I would often rush into decisions based on excitement or eagerness alone. While that can sometimes work, it's also costly when it doesn't. I've learned that developing a solid sixth sense in business doesn't mean abandoning caution—it means having the foresight to gather supporting evidence even when time is limited.

Let's take *Shark Tank* as an example again. During those three-minute pitches, I would get an immediate feeling about a product or idea. But instead of solely relying on that gut feeling, I'd ask targeted questions to verify my instincts: "Who's the competition? What's the profit margin? Do you have any testimonials?" By digging into key areas, I could quickly confirm or adjust my initial impression. That's an essential lesson for anyone developing their sixth sense: use it as a guide, but don't ignore the value of facts and verification.

In another instance, I remember being pitched a product that initially seemed like a clear winner. It was flashy, unique, and had a solid story. My instincts were saying "Yes," but something felt off about the numbers. After a bit more digging, I discovered some financial inconsistencies that would have made it a much riskier investment than I'd thought. My gut was still right about the product's potential, but that extra research saved me from a potentially huge financial pitfall.

THE "TEASE, PLEASE, & SEIZE" FRAMEWORK

One of my go-to approaches in making rapid evaluations is what I call the "Tease, Please, and Seize" framework. This is a process I've used to quickly assess and enhance any pitch or idea. It's a simple concept, but it's highly effective, especially when time is short.

1. Tease: This is the attention-grabber. Every product needs a clear, compelling hook that immediately captures the audience's interest. It's the "why should I care" factor. In a pitch, I look for something that stands out, whether it's a unique problem being solved or a captivating story.

2. Please: This step is about building trust and demonstrating value. I want to see proof. How does this product solve the problem? What benefits does it provide, and what is its unique selling point? Testimonials, endorsements, or evidence of effectiveness are crucial here.

3. Seize: Finally, this is the close, the irresistible offer. Every successful pitch should end with an opportunity that feels too good to pass up. Whether it's a limited-time deal, a free bonus, or a clear call to action, this is the part that pushes people to commit.

In my business, I've seen this process work time and time again, and it's something I instinctively apply when making quick decisions. For example, when evaluating a product on *Shark Tank*, I'd mentally run through the Tease, Please, and Seize steps to see if the entrepreneur was hitting each point effectively. If they could capture my attention, build credibility, and then close with a strong offer, they had my attention—and often, my investment.

THE TEN KEY STEPS TO CREATING YOUR PERFECT PITCH

While the "Tease, Please, and Seize" framework offers a quick, effective way to assess and enhance pitches, I've developed a detailed process for delivering a perfect pitch over my career. This process builds on capturing attention, demonstrating value, and making an irresistible offer by breaking each aspect into focused steps. Here are my **10 Steps to Creating the Perfect Pitch** when evaluating the thousands of pitches I receive and making the best business decisions:

1. Tease: Begin by "hooking" your audience. Present the problem in a relatable and attention-grabbing way to make your audience recognize the need for a solution.

2. Please: Describe how your product or service uniquely solves the problem introduced in the Tease step. Highlight its main features, benefits, and value.

3. Show in Action: Demonstrate the product in real-time, showcasing its multi-functionality to add value and prove it can deliver on its promise.

4. Add Value with "But Wait, There's More!": Offer additional incentives or bonuses to make the deal more appealing and emphasize why it's a no-brainer investment.

5. Provide Rock-Solid Testimonials: Share credible third-party endorsements (such as user, professional, or celebrity testimonials) to build trust and social proof and make your solution more persuasive.

6. Highlight Research & Competitive Analysis: Show you've done the groundwork, understand the competition, and know why your solution is uniquely positioned.

7. Reveal Your Dream Team: Introduce a qualified team to support your venture, which will reassure investors about the project's potential for success.

8. Explain Why You Need the Money: Detail how the funds will be used, why they're necessary, and how they'll drive the business forward, making it clear you have a well-thought-out plan.

9. Outline Your Marketing Plan: Present a structured strategy for reaching your target audience, generating buzz, and scaling, demonstrating that you have a clear path to market.

10. Ask for the Money: End with a strong call to action. Ask for the funding, equity, or commitment you need, making the offer irresistible and easy to say "yes" to.

These ten steps aren't just about following a formula; they're designed to develop and strengthen your intuitive ability to pitch effectively. By internalizing these steps, you'll refine your sixth sense for recognizing opportunities and cultivate a clear, repeatable process to capture investor interest and close deals with confidence.

NAVIGATING THE CHALLENGES OF PREJUDGMENT

One of the biggest challenges with the sixth sense is avoiding prejudgment. It's easy to fall into the trap of thinking you know everything about a product or person at first glance, but the sixth sense is about understanding beyond the surface. This was the case with the Great Wok of China, where I saw value others overlooked.

Prejudgment can kill opportunities, especially in a fast-paced environment. That's why I always recommend checking in with your sixth sense and asking yourself, "Am I giving this a fair chance, or am I making assumptions?" This habit has opened doors for me that might have otherwise remained closed, and it's an essential part of building a successful career in any field.

BUILDING YOUR SIXTH SENSE OVER TIME

Developing a sixth sense doesn't happen overnight. It's a process built on years of learning, documenting, and honing your instincts. Like musicians practice scales until they can play by ear, entrepreneurs practice decisions until they can "hear" the right choice. My journey as an entrepreneur, from launching Quantum International to scaling twenty businesses to $100 million each, taught me that repetition and refinement are essential to building this ability.

For example, in the early days of my career, I took on nearly every opportunity that came my way. I wanted to gain experience and learn as much as I could. But as my intuition sharpened, I became more selective. Now, I can recognize patterns much faster, and my sixth sense often picks up on cues that others might miss. This has allowed me to make decisions more confidently and quickly, freeing up time and resources for new ventures.

For anyone reading this, if you want to build your own sixth sense, reflect on past choices to identify successful patterns. Reflect on your past successes and failures, identify patterns, and use those insights to inform your future choices. With each decision, you'll better recognize what feels right and be more adept at trusting your intuition.

THE ROLE OF MENTORSHIP & A DREAM TEAM

While developing a sixth sense is essential, it's equally important to surround yourself with people who can complement and challenge your instincts. Throughout my career, I've benefited from having a "dream team" of experts, advisors, and mentors who bring diverse perspectives and insights to the table. Even the best intuition can benefit from an outside opinion, and having a trusted circle allows you to double-check your gut reactions with those you respect.

When I feel strongly about an opportunity, I often consult with other experts, asking them to play devil's advocate or give their honest take. Sometimes, a different perspective can illuminate potential risks or advantages that I hadn't considered. This helps me refine my sixth sense even further and provides a valuable safety net that I rely on to ensure I make the best decision possible.

Take the early days of *Shark Tank*, for example. We Sharks all have unique strengths and perspectives, and I often learned from how others approached a pitch. Watching Mark Cuban or Barbara Corcoran assess a deal with their own intuitive processes added to my toolkit and helped me see things from angles I hadn't previously considered. Developing a sixth sense is a personal journey, but input from a strong, diverse team can take it to new heights.

TRUSTING YOUR SIXTH SENSE

Intuition is an invaluable skill that takes time to develop but pays dividends in the long run. You can develop a sixth sense that guides you through your professional journey by tuning in to your own experiences, listening to your instincts, and backing them up with thoughtful research.

As Napoleon Hill wrote, the sixth sense is the final step in the journey toward mastering the mind. For me, this journey has spanned over four decades, thousands of pitches, and billions in sales. Each decision, each pitch, and each success has contributed to this intuitive ability, allowing me to make impactful choices quickly and effectively. But I've also learned that trusting this sixth sense means listening to the stories behind products, resisting snap judgments, and relying on a strong team for insights and validation.

So, as you embark on your own journey to develop the sixth sense, remember to trust your instincts, seek out mentors, and be open to the stories that might lead to your next big success. This is the art and science of intuitive decision-making, and in today's fast-paced business world, it's more essential than ever.

KEVIN HARRINGTON

Kevin Harrington is a pioneering entrepreneur and business leader with over four decades of experience. As one of the original "Sharks" on the Emmy-winning television show *Shark Tank*, Harrington has become a recognized authority in entrepreneurship, investing, and brand building. Known as the inventor of the infomercial and the "As Seen On TV" brand, Kevin revolutionized direct-to-consumer marketing, creating a global phenomenon that changed the way products are sold. He co-founded the Electronic Retailers Association (ERA). He was a founding board member of the Entrepreneurs' Organization (EO), which has grown to thousands of members across 45 countries, generating over $500 billion in member sales.

Kevin began his career in the early 1980s by investing $25,000 to launch Quantum International. This venture eventually generated $500 million annually on the New York Stock Exchange, driving its stock price from $1 to $20 per share. His next endeavor, HSN Direct, was a joint venture with the Home Shopping Network that generated hundreds of millions in sales. Throughout his career, Kevin has launched over 20 businesses that have surpassed $100 million in sales each and has introduced more than 500 products worldwide, amassing over $5 billion in total revenue.

Currently, Kevin operates a private consulting firm, leveraging his expertise to help companies expand distribution, strategize digital and media marketing, and build powerful celebrity partnerships. He is known for his ability to multiply the stock prices of companies he advises, and his influence has reached millions across various media platforms, including *The Wall Street Journal*, *Forbes*, *Inc.*, *USA Today*, and *CNBC*. As an author, Kevin shares his insights in bestselling books such as *Act Now: How I Turn Ideas into Million Dollar Products* and *Put a Shark in Your Tank*, as well as *the Secrets of Closing the Sale Master Class*, inspired by Zig Ziglar.

Kevin is one of the fan favorites at all of the Habitude Warrior Conferences. Kevin's enduring legacy in the entrepreneurial world combines his keen business acumen with an unmatched passion for innovation, making him one of today's most respected business mentors and thought leaders.

13 FEATURED CELEBRITY AUTHORS IN THE 13 STEPS TO RICHES

DR. DENIS WAITLEY ~ Author of *Psychology of Winning & The NEW Psychology of Winning—Top Qualities of a 21st Century Winner*, NASA's Performance Coach, Featured in *The Secret.* ~ www.DenisWaitley.com

SHARON LECHTER ~ 5 Time N.Y. Times Bestselling Author. Author of *Think and Grow Rich for Women*, Co-Author of *Exit Rich, Rich Dad Poor Dad, Three Feet from Gold, Outwitting the Devil* and *Success and Something Greater.* ~ www.SharonLechter.com

JIM CATHCART~ Bestselling Author of Relationship Selling and The Acorn Principle, among many others. Certified Speaking Professional (CSP) and Former President of the National Speakers Association (NSA).
~ www.Cathcart.com

MICHAEL E. GERBER ~ N.Y. Times Bestseller of the mega-bestselling theory for over two consecutive decades...*The E-Myth* Books.
~ www.MichaelEGerberCompanies.com

ERIK SWANSON ~ Multi-Time #1 International Bestselling Author, Award-Winning Speaker, Featured on TEDx Talks and Amazon Prime TV, Harvard University Keynote Guest Speaker. Founder & CEO of Habitude Warrior International & Integrity Publishing International.
~ www.SpeakerErikSwanson.com

MARIE DIAMOND ~ Featured in *The Secret*, Modern Day Spiritual Teacher, Inspirational Speaker, Feng Shui Master. ~ www.MarieDiamond.com

DAN CLARK ~ Award Winning Speaker, Speaker Hall of Fame, N.Y. Times Bestselling Author of *The Art of Significance*. ~ www.DanClark.com

ALEC STERN ~ America's Startup Success Expert, Co-Founder of Constant Contact, Speaker, Mentor, and Investor. ~ www.AlecSpeaks.com

LORAL LANGEMEIER ~ 5 Time N.Y. Times Bestselling Author, Featured in *The Secret*, Author of *The Millionaire Maker* and *YES! Energy - The Equation to Do Less, Make More*. ~ www.LoralLangemeier.com

DAME DORIA CORDOVA ~ CEO of Money & You, Excellerated Business School, Global Business Developer, Ambassador of New Education. ~ www.FridaysWithDoria.com

JOHN ASSARAF ~ Chairman & CEO NeuroGym, MrNeuroGym.com, New York Times bestselling author of *Having It All*, *Innercise*, and *The Answer.* Also featured in *The Secret.* ~ www.JohnAssaraf.com

KEVIN HARRINGTON ~ Original "Shark" on the hit TV show Shark Tank, Creator of the Infomercial, Pioneer of the As Seen on TV brand, Co-Author of Mentor to Millions. ~ www.KevinHarrington.TV

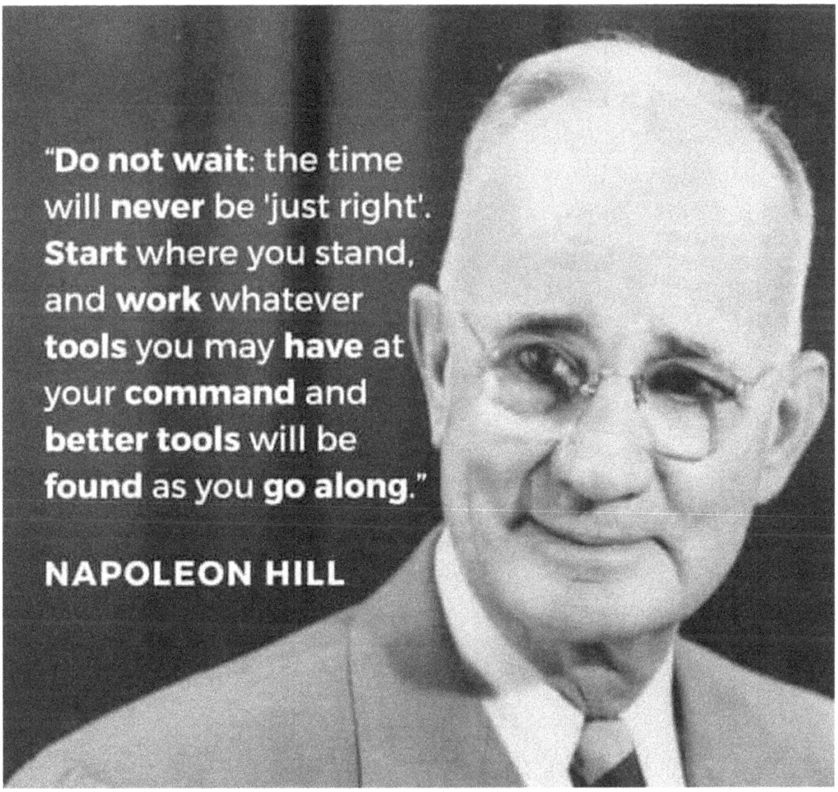

DR. MICHELLE MRAS

Michelle is an International TEDx Speaker, Award-Winning Keynote Speaker, Communication Trainer, Success Coach, Co-Host of the *Denim & Pearls* and *Amplifluence* podcast, the Author of *Eat, Drink and Be Mary: A Glimpse Into a Life Well Lived,* and *It's Not Luck: Overcoming You,* and Host of the *MentalShift* show on The New Channel (TNC), Philippines.

Michelle is a survivor of multiple life challenges, including a Traumatic Brain Injury and her current battle with Breast Cancer. She guides her clients to recognize the innate gifts within them, to stop apologizing for what they are not, and step into who they truly are. She accomplishes this through one-on-one and group coaching, training events, keynote talks, her books, podcasts, and MentalShift television show.

Awarded the Inspirational Women of Excellence Award from the Women Economic Forum, New Delhi, India; the John Maxwell Team Culture Award for Positive Attitude; She has been featured on hundreds of Podcasts, radio programs, several magazines, and lends her voice to audiobooks and has a habit of breaking out into song.

Michelle's driving thought is that every day is a gift. Tomorrow is never promised. Every moment is an opportunity to be the best version of you... Unapologetically!

www.MichelleMras.com

INTEGRITY PUBLISHING INTERNATIONAL

Integrity Publishing International is one of the world's most trusted hybrid publishing houses, dedicated to helping authors share their stories with authenticity, excellence, and integrity. Founded by Erik "Mr. Awesome" Swanson, a 33-Time #1 Bestselling Author, international speaker, and award-winning mentor, Integrity Publishing has guided more than 500 authors to achieve #1 Bestseller status in over 13 countries—and continues to empower writers across the globe.

Our mission is simple: to help you publish your story and become the author you were meant to be. Whether you're a first-time writer or a seasoned professional, our hands-on, step-by-step publishing programs make it easy to bring your message to life. With our Half Pack, Full Pack, and Ultimate Pack programs, authors can publish eBook, paperback, hardcover, and even audiobook formats—distributed through over 45,000 booksellers worldwide, including Amazon and Barnes & Noble.

Integrity Publishing is proud to offer more than publishing—we provide mentorship, community, and world-class resources to help every author shine. Our Authors Resource Page, ongoing training, and editorial support ensure your voice is heard, your story is polished, and your impact is global.

Led by an extraordinary team of professionals, we are committed to serving authors with heart, purpose, and excellence.

Join the hundreds of voices who have become #1 Bestselling Authors with Integrity Publishing International.

Your story matters. Let's share it with the world!

Team@IntegrityPub.com
www.IntegrityPublishingInternational.com